Mastering Unreal Engine

Mastering Unreal Engine

A Beginner's Guide

Edited by Sufyan bin Uzayr

CRC Press
Taylor & Francis Group
Boca Raton London New York

CRC Press is an imprint of the
Taylor & Francis Group, an **informa** business

First edition published 2022
by CRC Press
6000 Broken Sound Parkway NW, Suite 300, Boca Raton, FL 33487-2742

and by CRC Press
2 Park Square, Milton Park, Abingdon, Oxon, OX14 4RN

CRC Press is an imprint of Taylor & Francis Group, LLC

© 2022 Sufyan bin Uzayr

ISBN: 9781032103143 (hbk)
ISBN: 9781032103136 (pbk)
ISBN: 9781003214731 (ebk)

DOI: 10.1201/9781003214731

Typeset in Minion
by KnowledgeWorks Global Ltd.

Contents

About the Editor

Sufyan bin Uzayr is a writer, coder, and entrepreneur with more than a decade of experience in the industry. He has authored several books in the past, pertaining to a diverse range of topics, ranging from History to Computers/IT.

Sufyan is the Director of Parakozm, a multinational IT company specializing in EdTech solutions. He also runs Zeba Academy, an online learning and teaching vertical with a focus on STEM fields.

Sufyan specializes in a wide variety of technologies, such as JavaScript, Dart, WordPress, Drupal, Linux, and Python. He holds multiple degrees, including ones in Management, IT, Literature, and Political Science.

Sufyan is a digital nomad, dividing his time between four countries. He has lived and taught in universities and educational institutions around the globe. Sufyan takes a keen interest in technology, politics, literature, history, and sports, and in his spare time, he enjoys teaching coding and English to young students.

Learn more at sufyanism.com.

About the Editor

CHAPTER 1

Introduction to Unreal Engine

Epic Games released the original Unreal Engine in 1998. This engine's primary advantage was that thanks to UnrealScript, the engine became fairly popular with the community since it made modding quite easy and accessible. Then, in 2002, Epic launched Unreal Engine 2, which was a significant upgrade over the previous engine. It came with UnrealEd 2 (and subsequently, UnrealEd 3), a level editor you could use to construct Unreal levels. This, in conjunction with UnrealScript, may be used to develop entirely new games. The engine outperformed its predecessor in terms of rendering, physics, and collision. It also supported the current generation platforms at the time, particularly the PlayStation 2, Xbox, and GameCube. Epic launched Unreal 3, its next and most successful and extensively used engine, in 2006. In terms of technology, it was

DOI: 10.1201/9781003214731-1   **1**

a huge step forward. This was when Unreal Engine gained traction. However, Kismet was probably the most crucial feature given by Unreal Engine 3.

Kismet is a highly effective visual scripting tool. It works by having multiple nodes that may be linked to make a logical sequence, similar to a flowchart. The most excellent aspect about Kismet is that you don't need any programming skills to use it.

Kismet allows you to create a complete game without writing a single line of code.

It is a handy tool for artists and designers since it allows them to create rapid prototypes or experiment with a specific feature without relying on programmers. We have now arrived in a more recent epoch. Epic introduced Unreal 4 in February 2012, and it was ultimately launched on March 19, 2014. It has been in development since 2003. This Engine was a significant improvement over the previous one. For one thing, it completely replaced UnrealScript with C++. If you wanted to change the engine to create your game in earlier versions of Unreal, you had to do it using UnrealScript, which entailed learning a new language.

However, if you want to alter the Engine, you may now do so using C++. This was a significant step forward for engine programmers since it allowed them to change and tweak everything they wanted using a language they already knew and loved. Not only that, but the engine's source code is accessible for developers to download from the GitHub site. This implies that developers have complete control over the engine and may change almost everything, including the physics, graphics, and user interface (UI).

It also has a feature known as the Hot Reload. Normally, if you wish to make changes to a game's code, you must first stop the game, make the necessary modification, and then restart it to see how it impacts the game. On the other hand, the hot reload option allows you to make adjustments without stopping or halting it. Any changes you make to the game's code are immediately updated, and you can view the results in real time.

Unreal four also allows you to create games on various platforms, including Xbox One, PlayStation 4 (including Project Morpheus), Windows PC, Linux, Mac OS X, HTML 5, iOS, and Android. It also supports the Oculus Rift. Another significant modification implemented by Epic is the licensing mechanism geared toward smaller, independent developers. To be more explicit, to license Unreal Development Kit (UDK), the previous version of Unreal Engine, developers had to pay a $99 licensing fee and 25% of royalties collected after the firm had generated at least $50,000 in sales. However, in Unreal 4, the framework has been altered.

Unreal Engine has been free to use and download since 2015. There is no license cost, no membership price, nothing. You may download it, create a game on it, and publish it without paying a dime for the engine. After you generate more than $3,000 in income, you only pay 5% of the royalties.

The Marketplace is another fantastic element of Unreal 4. The Marketplace is an excellent location for purchasing and uploading assets. 3D Models, Materials, Animations, Sound Effects, Premade Games, and so on are examples of assets. This is also fantastic news for prospective developers who lack the necessary money and labor to create these assets. They may simply purchase the required components from the Marketplace and incorporate them into their game. Developers can also make money by uploading their work to the Marketplace.

Unreal Engine is a complete development suite for anyone working with real-time technology. It provides flexibility and power to artists across sectors to produce cutting-edge entertainment, captivating visualizations, and immersive virtual environments. Epic Games' Unreal Engine is a prominent and extensively used gaming engine.

It is utilized in many current AAA games, including Epic's battle royale shooter Fortnite and other popular titles like Psyonix's "Rocket League."

It enables creation on various platforms ranging from PC to consoles such as the PS4, Xbox One, and Nintendo Switch. Because of its ability to function across platforms, this is one of the reasons it is so popular.

More skilled programmers can create scripts that run in the game engine using the C++ language. More inexperienced developers may use its vital blueprints, which are effectively premade chunks of code that we can apply to our objects to build interactions. This method allows us to create rudimentary interaction in our VR scenarios, such as the ability to pick up or toss items. It also has sophisticated material and animation capabilities for artists, allowing us to create complex scenarios quickly. Setting up some of these features may appear overwhelming at first, but numerous examples are provided to modify the parameters until we achieve the desired result simply.

On top of all of these capabilities, there is a wealth of documentation to assist you in learning the system.

The fact that Unreal Engine is entirely free to use is a significant advantage. There is no upfront charge to utilize Unreal, whether you are a hobbyist developer or a AAA business. Instead, they make their money through a royalty arrangement that pays them 5% of all gaming revenues over $3,000 every quarter.

WHAT TO EXPECT?

Learning to utilize a game engine may be difficult; you don't know where to start, and UE4 is no exception. However, after you've mastered it, you'll immediately realize how powerful and intuitive it truly is. And what better way to learn how to utilize a game engine than to create a game with it? This book will teach you all you need to know to design games for Android devices using UE4 and create a fully working game in the process.

The rationale for this is simple: simply discussing and showing UE4's capabilities one at a time is ineffective when learning how to create a game. However, explaining those characteristics by incorporating them into a game would be far more successful since you would have a more excellent grasp of how each element influences the game and each other. The game we'll be making in this guide is called Bloques, and it's a first-person puzzle game in which the player's primary goal is to solve a series of riddles to proceed.

The riddles get increasingly intricate and challenging to complete as the player goes. The game's scope will be four rooms, each having a riddle that the player must solve to proceed to the next area.

The reason for selecting a puzzle game is that puzzle games have more complex systems in terms of programming and level design. In the tutorial context, concepts like blueprint programming and level technique will be much better taught through a puzzler.

UE CHARACTERISTICS AND FREQUENT USAGE

Unreal Engine would not have survived as long as it has if it wasn't continuously introducing new features to stay ahead of the competition. Its combination of artistic and development-focused tools provides us with total creative freedom.

For materials and rendering, it employs the widely used PBR process. When combined with dynamic or baked-in shadows and lighting, this results in some incredible photorealistic material that continues to run in real time. The Blueprints tool, which I described before, allows you to create basic scripts that communicate with one another. This is all done using a visual interface, so even if you've never programmed before, a few brief lessons will have you well on your way to creating a functional game. When Epic published "Unreal" (the game) in 1998, there were difficulties with its multiplayer features, which were still instead cutting edge at the time.

They spent over a year fixing this, and it finally became a new game called "Unreal Tournament" in 1999. This multiplayer architecture is now one of the key selling features. They made changes as recently as September 2017 that allow up to 100 distinct people to join and play together in a single game, implying that the possibilities are nearly infinite.

Unreal Engine has a decent physics engine that supports soft-body physics, particle effects, and more basic stuff like gravity. The framework is simple to use for creating items such as a swing that responds to being pushed. It's all quite simple once you've mastered the UI.

You have an incredible amount of leeway here. Once you've imported your texture maps from another application, such as Substance Painter, you may utilize the hundreds of different material blueprints to endlessly customize the ultimate result to obtain precisely what you want. There are additional tools built in that make it much easier to design for virtual or augmented reality.

In recent years, the growth in popularity of VR has been unmistakable; thus, having access to an engine that can quickly help you develop content for these platforms, such as the Oculus Rift and HTC Vive, is always beneficial. Unreal Engine also has tools that allow you to design your landscape easily. You may use your mouse to paint in your materials and blend them to create grass, for example, progressively bleed into a concrete walkway.[1]

Then, using meshes of trees and grass, you may paint in entire forests or patches of flowers. If you use the plant models included with Unreal Engine, you can create whole outdoor scenes in a matter of minutes, and they are fully optimized to run in your game. The content browser is an essential component of the UI. It allows you to rapidly

---

[1] https://conceptartempire.com/what-is-unreal-engine/, Concept Art

explore your scene's entire file hierarchy to discover different assets and drag them directly into the viewport.

This enables several simplified procedures, which makes working with the engine a delight. The marketplace is the last aspect worth mentioning. This is a collection of assets created by Epic and other Unreal Engine developers. This marketplace allows you to download more art assets and entire development builds to which you can then contribute. You may also use them to investigate tools utilized by a developer to understand them better.

System Needs

Before you go ahead and download UE4, be sure you have a machine capable of running it in the first place! UE4 is compatible with both Windows and Mac OS X. The system requirements for each are as follows:

- 64-bit Windows 7/8 (Or Mac OS X 10.9.2 or later).

- .NET Framework 4.0.

- DirectX ten (Mac: OpenGL 3.3).

- The RAM capacity of 8 GB.

- Quad-core Intel or AMD processor with a speed of 2.5 GHz or higher.

- AMD Radeon 6870 HD series or higher.

- NVIDIA GeForce 470 GTXabove.

- A minimum of 9 GB of hard disc space (8 GB for Mac OS X).

DOWNLOADING AND INSTALLING

The procedure of downloading and installing UE4 is quite simple; simply follow these steps:

1. Navigate to the Unreal Engine official website (https://www.unrealengine.com/).

   The following is a snapshot of the home page:

   Everything you need to know about UE4 can be found here, including the most recent news, the most recent engine version, blog updates, Marketplace entries, and so on. The engine has been available as a free download since 2015.

   In addition to the UE4 homepage, you should go to https://docs.unrealengine.com/latest/INT/. It's jam-packed with documentation and video lessons on how to utilize UE4. Epic has a big, active, and kind community that is always eager to help anybody in need via the forums.

2. Click on the download button that is on the right side of the screen from the main page. Clicking on

it will take you to the subscription page, which is seen below:

3. To download and install UE4, you must first establish an account.

    Simply fill in the needed information and follow the steps to develop an account with Epic Games.

4. Sign in to get the Engine Launcher. You can view your profile, billing history, prior transactions, and so on, from your account page.

5. Now that you've created an account, you may download UE4. Depending on your configuration, you

may download either the Windows or Mac version. To download, go to Latest Download and click on the Download button. The Engine Launcher will be downloaded.

6. To start the installer, just double-click Unreal-EngineInstaller-*version number*.msi on Windows or UnrealEngineInstaller-*version number*.dmg on Mac. Install the Engine Launcher by following the on-screen instructions.

7. Once installation is finished, launch the Launcher.

8. When you log in, the Engine Launcher will appear. We'll go through it and its features in more depth later, but for now, all you need to do is go to Library and click on the Add Versions button next to Engines. This will result in the creation of a slot. You may choose a version number from the version dropdown in the version slot you created, then click the Install button, and the version of UE4 you choose will begin downloading.

9. That's all! You have successfully downloaded and installed UE4 on your computer (or Mac). Simply click the Launch button in the top-left corner of the Launcher, underneath the user name, to start the engine, and you're ready to go. If necessary, you can also run older versions of the engine. Clicking on the downward arrow next to the Launch button will reveal a menu with all of the engine's versions listed; simply click on the version you want to run to launch it.

10. Alternatively, we can click on the Library button and select which engine is to run from there. All of the versions installed on our system will be listed, and you can simply launch any version from the list by clicking on the Launch button.

The Directory Structure of Windows

The default installation location for UE4 is C:\Program Files\Unreal Engine\.

You can alter this throughout the installation process if you like. When you open the directory, you'll notice that each engine version has its folder.

Assume you have UE4 versions 4.1, 4.2, and 4.3 installed on your machine. There are three distinct folders for each of the three versions, 4.1, 4.2, and 4.3. Each version of the Engine is given its folder. Aside from that, there are two other folders: DirecXRedist and Launcher.

DirectXRedist FOR WINDOWS

DirectXRedist is the location of the DirectX files. The folder also includes the installation file, which may be used to install DirectX.

Launcher

The Launcher folder includes all of the Engine Launcher's files. The Launcher folder is divided into the following subfolders:

- **Backup:** UE4 offers a fantastic tool that allows you to generate backups of your work. If a developer makes an unfixable or challenging error, or if the Engine crashes in the middle of development, instead of having them redo all of their work, a backup of their work will be saved in the Backup folder, allowing them to start up where they left off.

- **Engine:** This folder includes all of the engine's code, libraries, and data.

- **PatchStaging:** Epic will occasionally release a new version of UE4. The most recent version available as of 2022 is 4.27. (At the time of writing, the preview version of 4.8 is available.) When you download UE4, all of the data from the currently downloaded version/versions of UE4 is saved in the PatchStaging folder.

- **VaultCache:** All we need to know for now is that anything we buy in the Marketplace is stored in the Vault. The VaultCache includes all of the cache files for the purchased items.

4.X FOLDERS

Before we go into the 4.X files, you should know that all UE4 versions (4.1, 4.2, 4.3, and so forth) function independently of one another. This implies that you do not need the prior version to run the subsequent versions.

For example, if you want to run version 4.4, you don't need to download versions 4.0, 4.1, 4.2, or 4.3 beforehand. We may download and use version 4.4 without any issues. This is why there is a separate subdirectory for each Unreal 4 version; each version is regarded as a unique object.

Although distinct, all 4.X folders have the same set of subfolders; thus, they are grouped. The subfolders are as follows:

- **Engine:** This folder, like the Launcher's Engine folder, includes all of the Engine's source code, libraries, assets, map files, and other files.

- **Sample Maps:** UE4 includes two sample maps: Minimal Default and Starter Map. This folder has all of the material, including assets, blueprints, and other files.

- **Templates:** UE4 has templates for various game genres, including first-person, third-person, 2D side scroller, top-down, and many more. This folder contains all of the content for each of these genres and the source code.

THE ENGINE STARTER

The Engine Launcher is a window that appears once you have started the engine. It is jam-packed with features and information that can be highly beneficial to you. First, we'll look at the Engine Launcher's UI, including its breakdown, where everything is placed, and functionality.

When you open the Engine Launcher, there are three options in the top left: Unreal Tournament, Unreal Engine, and Fortnite. The tab of Unreal Engine is open by default, and it contains the contents of the previous screenshot. The Unreal Tournament area contains information and links to the most recent Unreal Tournament game.

MARKETPLACE

Developers can purchase assets from the Marketplace. Developers who lack the workforce or money to develop assets might buy them and include them in their game.

Meshes, materials, animation sets, rigged characters, audio files, sound effects, projects, and tutorials are just a few examples. Certain products in the Marketplace, such as those created by Epic, are free. They are primarily instructional project files with a sample level already set up to demonstrate various UE4 capabilities.

All the level designs are also put up and implemented in these project files, so users can view them and experiment with them until they get the hang of it. Other goods in the Marketplace that users developed are not free. For your convenience, the materials available for purchase are neatly organized into categories based on the type of content.

In addition to purchasing goods, you can also submit your work to the Marketplace and make money from it. The Submit your content hyperlink in the top-right corner of the Marketplace screen will take you to Epic's Call for Submission website. All information about submitting material may be found on the Call for Submissions page. It also includes the Marketplace Business Terms, which include how the money from sales will be shared, how you will be paid, when you will be paid, and so on. It also consists of the Marketplace Submission Guidelines, which describe the submission procedure, what you need to provide, screenshot resolution, and more. Posting on the Forums will also provide you with further information on the submission procedure and comments on your material.

LIBRARY

The Library is where you can find all versions of UE4, your projects, and any goods you've purchased from the Marketplace. The Library is divided into three sections: Engine Versions, My Projects, and Vault. The Engine Versions section lists all of the UE4 versions that are presently installed on your system.

You can start any of the Engine versions listed below. You may also download the most recent version or older versions. Simply click on Add Versions at the top of the panel, right next to Engines Versions, to do so. When you click on it, a space will be created for the version you want to download.

The Add Versions button added a space for the most recent version of Unreal 4, which is 4.8.0.

To download, simply click the Download button, and the download will begin.

You may also uninstall UE4 versions that you no longer need. For example, if we have the most recent version, it is natural to delete prior or older versions of the engine to free up space on your hard disc.

To do so, simply move your mouse over the top-left corner of the version slot until you see an x. When we know the x, merely click on it, and the matching version of UE4 will be downloaded. Must be uninstalled. Uninstalling can also be accomplished by clicking on the downward arrow button next to Launch, which brings up a drop-down menu from which you may pick Remove. The Engine Launcher will uninstall that version. My project is the second section of the Library. All of the projects you've made are presented in this area. The projects are alphabetically organized. The search bar is located in the upper-right corner.

Because there are few project files in the above picture, it is simple to locate a particular project. However, if you have a lot of projects, it may be more challenging to find the one you're searching for. In such instance, put the project's name into the Search Projects tab, and it will discover it for you. You can tell the version of the engine a project was developed in by looking at the bottom-right corner of its thumbnail. For example, in the above picture, the project Effects was developed using UE4 version 4.0. When you open the project file, the Launcher launches UE4 version 4.0. If you do not have the matching version, you will be prompted to choose the installed version you want to run the project file when you launch it. After you've made your selection, it'll modify the project to be compatible with the version you've chosen and launch it. However, while converting a project, you should always be cautious because specific unforeseen difficulties may arise. It is recommended that you make a backup copy of the project before converting it.

Double-click on the image to start a project. Aside from opening a project, you may also do additional operations with the projects. A menu appears when you right-click on the thumbnail. The project will be deleted if you click the Delete button.

The clone will make a clone of the project file, and Show in Folder will open the folder containing all of the project files on your machine.

Then there's the Vault. The Vault holds all of the things you've purchased from the Marketplace.

CHAPTER 2

Start of the Work with Unreal Engine

We have everything prepared and are excited to go now that we can download and install UE4. However, one crucial subject must be addressed before we begin developing our game, and that is the Editor.

All of the magic happens in the Editor. And that is where the game is created. Before we proceed, we must understand the Editor, its functions, the user interface, and how to move around it. As a result, this chapter will walk you through it.

We will discuss the following topics:

- Who is the Editor?

- Its graphical user interface.

- Using the Editor to navigate.

- Controls and hotkeys.

DOI: 10.1201/9781003214731-2

INTRODUCTION TO THE EDITOR

You create the game with the Editor. The Editor is used to apply all of the assets you generate for your game. The Editor is where you build up your environment and levels and test all of the code sequences you write; it's also where you test, debug, and package your game.

Needless to say, before we go, we must grasp what the Editor is, become acquainted with its user interface, and learn how to move around it.

Unreal Project Browser

- Unless you have launched a project directly from the library, the Unreal Project Browser will start when you run UE4 through the Engine Launcher. In the Unreal Project Browser, you may see a list of all the Unreal projects you've already made and open any of them. You may also start a new project from this page.

- At the top there are two tabs, right below the tab bar, titled Projects and New Project. Each of these tabs has features that we will go through.

- We can see and open any project you've saved on our system under the Projects tab. The search bar is located at the top of the page. If we have a lot of projects and are having trouble finding one, simply type the name of the project we want to open in the search field, and it will list projects that match the name provided.

- The Refresh button is located to the right of the search bar. If we've made any purchases through the marketplace, they won't show up in the browser. Click the Refresh button to refresh the project list. The Marketplace button is next to the Refresh button; clicking on this will take us to the Engine Launchers Marketplace panel.

- The My Projects area is located beneath the search bar and displays all of the projects we've made. The Samples section is located beneath My Projects. Any gameplay or engine features samples that you may purchase from the Marketplace are listed here.

- The Samples section comes next. Everything you get from Engine Feature Samples, Example Game Projects, and other sources is presented here. The procedure of upgrading and degrading projects that we mentioned before also applies to these project files.

- Click on a project to open it, and the selected project will be highlighted in yellow. After we've chosen it, click the Open button to start it. If we need to launch a project that isn't listed in My Projects, just click the Browse button, search for the project file, and execute it. Finally, in the bottom-left corner of the window, there is a little checkbox labeled Always load the last project on startup. If you check the option, the previous project opened will be launched immediately when we load UE4.

- Now, we'll go on to the New Project panel. Depending on the sort of game we wish to create, you may select from various templates. There are templates for first-person games, puzzle games, side scroller games, and vehicle games. Blueprint and C++ templates are the two types of templates available. Blueprint projects do not necessitate any prior programming knowledge on the part of the user.

- The blueprint may be used to create all of the game's features, and the template also includes the entire set of blueprints needed for particular game modes such as camera, controls, physics, and so on. C++ projects, on the other hand, require the developers' knowledge of C++. These projects offer the fundamental structure for that specific template upon which the developers may build the game. Choosing Blueprint projects is advantageous for developers who lack programming skills because it facilitates development.

- However, while Blueprint is a fantastic tool, it is not as adaptable as code. When you code, we have more control over the engine, and we may even alter it to meet our needs. It also implies that our game will be more optimized. Developers may use the blueprint to implement functionality if necessary.

- A project is shown to the right of the project list, along with a description of it. After we've decided on the template to use, we may make a few options before starting the project. First and foremost, we have the chance to develop our game on PC/console or mobile/tablet hardware.

- When we launch the project, this will configure items like controls. Following that, you may choose the game's rendering quality. We have the choice of selecting between highest qualities or scalable. Although it is reasonable that we want our game to appear beautiful, we must keep in mind that mobile devices have limits. It is recommended that we use Scalable while creating for mobile devices.

- The contrast between Scalable and Maximum Quality is that the engine config files in Scalable are designed to provide the most outstanding performance. This means that some of the more expensive features, such as anti-aliasing and motion blur, are disabled by default. Lastly, one may pick whether or not to use the beginning content (which includes materials, objects, audio files, textures, and so on) while creating the project.

- After we've chosen these settings, you may specify where our project will be saved. In the left bar, the location and name of the folder where the project will be stored are presented. We may change it to whatever we like. You may change the name of the project in the right bar. Finally, once we've configured all of these parameters, just click the Create Project button to launch the Editor.

USER INTERFACE

The Editor will appear when we have started or created a new project. When we open the program, we will get the following screen:

The Editor is where you will design your game. Even though the Editors user interface is well organized, there are a lot of buttons, options, and panels. To simplify the user interface, we will break the Editor into sections and then go through each area individually.

The Menu Bar and the Tab Bar

The project's name, MyProject2, is written in light gray on the right side of the tab bar. The Send Quick Feedback button, which resembles a chat bubble, is next to the project's name. Do we want to offer Epic some good or bad comments on the Editor? We can do so by pressing this button. Simply clicking on the symbol will bring up a menu that may offer excellent or negative comments and ask Epic questions.

After you've made your selection, a window appears in which you may specify the nature of the feedback, followed by your opinions.

After we've finished writing your feedback, click Send to send it to Epic.

The Show Available Tutorials button, which, when pressed, displays a box in which we may pick whatever tutorial want to watch. There are tutorials accessible within the Editor. When we click the button, a new window appears, displaying all of the available tutorials. The menu bar is located beneath the tab bar. It includes all of the common commands and tools that are available in all apps.

- **File:** From here, you may create, open, and save levels/ maps, as well as create or open projects (creating or opening a new project closes the current project and reopens the Editor). We may also bundle your game from this page. Click on File, hover over Package Product, open another menu, select the platform we want to package our game, and follow the steps to finish the process. There are various options and build parameters that may configure here, which we will go over in more detail in later chapters.

- **Edit:** From the Edit menu, you may undo or redo the previous action, as well as cut, copy, paste, and duplicate any item (or collection of objects) you have selected. From here, we can also access the Editor settings. Simply choose Editor Preferences from the Edit menu. This will open a new window where we may configure settings such as turning on/off autosaves, adjusting the frequency of autosaves, modifying or assigning hotkeys, and changing the measurement units (centimeters, meters, or kilometers). More preferences options are available, so feel free to explore and modify them to suit our game. Finally, you may configure the open at the moment project's parameters. The Project Settings option is just underneath Editor Preferences; clicking on it displays the Project Settings window. In the Project Settings box, you may configure the project's description (including adding a thumbnail, a description, and a project ID), how the game will be packed, and which devices the project will support.

- **Window:** The Editor window may be completely customized. Aside from the tab and menu bar, all other windows in the Editor may be modified to your liking. The above screenshot depicts the Editor's default layout. You may add, delete, and rearrange any number of windows.

Simply follow these procedures to do so:

1. Place your cursor on the tab of the window that you want to relocate.

2. Click and hold the tab's left mouse button.

3. Drag the window to the desired location.

4. When you release the left mouse button, the window will be set.

We may not always be able to locate the Windows tab. For example, the Viewport lacks a tab. This is because its tab is hidden. Click on the yellow arrow in the top-left corner of the window to reveal it.

With the above in mind, the Windows menu is only for that. If you want to add another window to your Editor, simply open the Windows menu, pick the window you want to add, and click on it. When you do this, the window will open, and you may move and position it wherever you like.

The Window menu may come in handy if we're utilizing a dual-screen because there's room for extra windows.

- **Help:** Epic has made every effort to ensure that the lessons offered by them and the community are always easily available, whether through their website, the Engine Launcher, or the Editor itself. The Help menu is analogous to the Learn part of the Engine Launcher in that it contains links to all of the UE4 tutorials and documentation. The Search for Help bar is located in the upper-right corner of the menu bar.

Do we need to find a specific tutorial without having to go through the entire Help section? In that case, type in the name of the topic we wish to find tutorials on, and it will show matching results.

TOOLBAR

The toolbar is positioned right behind the tab and menu bar.

It gives you rapid access to the most frequently used commands and actions.

- **Save:** The Save button is located on the far left of the screen. Any developer understands the significance of this function. Because a single crash might wipe out all of your work, it is placed on the toolbar for easy access.

- **Source Control:** From here, you may activate or disable source control, which is disabled by default. When working in a team, source control is an essential tool. It is a way of keeping track of any modifications made to a file and regulating the program version. When a file is updated, the team may examine the modified files and, if necessary, share the changes for others to see. To activate it, click the button to reveal a dropdown menu and select Connect to Source. A new window will open, prompting you to choose a supplier. Choose the one you want and then click Accept Settings. Once enabled, you may view any changes made by other team members and post any changes you've made yourself.

- **Content:** The Content button launches the Content Browser. This is comparable to Unreal Engine 3's Content Browser. So, if we're already familiar with it, we should be OK with the updated version. For those who have never used Unreal Engine 3, the Content Browser is where we can find all of your assets, code, levels, and anything else.

- **Marketplace:** We've suddenly realized that you need an asset or assets for our game; instead of opening the Engine Launcher again, click on this button to get to the Engine Launcher's Marketplace area, where we may explore purchasing the needed item or things.

- **Settings:** This is identical to the Unreal Engine 3 Info settings. It lists the Editor's most frequently used settings. Toggling on/off actor snapping, allowing/disallowing selection of transparent objects, allowing/disallowing group selection, and other options are available here. It is also worth noting that the Engine's visual parameters, such as resolution, texture rendering quality, anti-aliasing, and others, maybe altered here.

- **Blueprints:** Since Chapter 3 is dedicated to Blueprint as it is an essential and widely utilized feature in UE4. From this page, you can access the Blueprint Editor.

- **Matinee:** Another important and widely used tool provided by UE4 that allows you to build cinematics and other effects in Unreal Matinee. Unreal Matinee may be accessed from this page.

- **Build:** UE4's build function is critical. The Engine precomputes lighting and visibility data, produces navigational networks, and changes geometry as we develop our level.

- **Play:** When we press the Play button, the game usually launches in the viewport, allowing us to test our level and ensure that everything is working correctly. When we start the game, the Play button is swapped by the three remaining buttons.

- **Pause:** Pressing this button brings the gaming session to a halt. You can restart or skip a frame when paused.

- **Stop:** This button terminates the game session and returns you to the editing mode.

- **Eject:** When you press the Play button, you assume control of a character. When you click Eject, you no longer have control over it and may move it about in the Viewport. You may change the settings for Play by clicking on the downward-facing arrow adjacent to the button, which opens the Play menu.

- **Launch:** After think game is complete and ready to be ported, click the Launch button to cook, package, and launch the project into an executable application file (dependent on the machine you choose to release your game on).

VIEWPORT

The Viewport, located in the center of the Editor, is where we build and watch our game. Your assets are all put and combined here to form your planet. 'Let's take a closer look at the Viewport. To navigate about, hold down the left or right mouse button and utilize the W, S, A, and D keys. Left-click on an object to select it. The Viewports toolbar is located at the top, with a little on the left and some on the right.

Let's look at each of these tools individually:

- **Viewport Options:** The Viewport Options may be found at the far left of the toolbar, indicated by the downward pointing arrow. When you select it, a menu appears with options for seeing the Viewport and what you want to see in it. You can, for example, select Game Mode, which presents the scenario as it would appear in the game. This implies that items like volumes, hidden actors, and actor symbols (for example, four actor icons in the above picture) are all concealed. There's also Immersive Mode, which expands the Viewport to fill the whole screen. Other settings are available under the Viewport Options menu, so take a look around.

- **Viewport Type:** The Viewport Type menu is next. Viewports are classified into two types: perspective and orthographic. The complete 3D view, inside which we can see the scene in three dimensions, is the perspective view. Orthographic view allows us to see the world in two sizes, along with the XZ (front), YZ (side), or XY plane (top).

- **View Mode:** There are several modes in which we can view your environment. By selecting the View Mode button, you may explore all of UE4's available view modes. The method is set to Lit by default. We may view how the levels look with all the light actors inside the scene in this mode. We may change the setting to Unlit, which, as the name implies, depicts the scene without any illumination. Another option we may select is Wireframe, which displays the wireframes of the actors in the scenario.

- **Show:** From here, you can choose which actors you wish to see or conceal in your scenario. When we open the menu, we'll see a list of things with check-boxes next to them. If we check the box, those sorts of actors will be visible in the scenario. If we leave the option unchecked, certain kinds of actors will be concealed.

- **Transform Tools:** Let's navigate to the right side of the toolbar and choose Transform Tools. First, we have the transform tools, which are represented by three icons. On an actor, three transform actions may be done. The first action is to translate, changing an actor's location (or coordinates) in our environment. The second action rotates, which revolves an actor around the x, y, or z axes. The third action is scale, which refers to raising or decreasing the size of an item. We may pick the action to conduct by selecting one of the Transform Tools.

- **Coordinate System:** A next item on the Viewport Toolbar is the Coordinate System, represented by a globe-shaped icon. Any transform operation takes to happen in one of two coordinate systems: global and local. We may switch between them by clicking on the button. The symbol will be a globe if the global coordinate system is activated. When we choose the local coordinate system, the icon will be a cube. When the local coordinate system is enabled, the axes around which you execute a transform operation will align with the rotation of the actor. When the global coordinate system is activated, it will not align with the rotation of the actors but will instead align with the world. The local coordinate system is active on the left, and the global coordinate system is active on the right.

- **Surface Snapping, Grid Snapping, and Grid Snap Value:** The following three tools all have something to do with the translate operation. Therefore they're grouped together.

  When the surface snapping tool is enabled, the actor will snap to surfaces (BSPs, other Actors' surfaces, and so on) when translated. It is represented by an icon in the shape of a curved line with an arrow perpendicular to it. This is useful when we need to position actors on the ground. Just make sure the actor's pivot is at the bottom, as this is the point where the surfaces snap together. When Grid Snapping is enabled (indicated by a grid-shaped icon), the actor moves in particular values when translated. Consider the globe to be a grid, with each cell having a specific size. If you translate an actor while it is active, it will snap to this grid. This is very useful in level design when you need exact actor placement with everything correctly spaced or aligned. The Grid Snap

Value option allows you to choose the value by which these actors will shift.

- **Rotation Grid Snapping and Rotation Grid Snap Value:** The following two tools are identical to Grid Snapping, except for the rotation action. When activated, the actor will rotate in predefined increments (for example, 10 degrees). The Rotation Grid Snap Value option allows you to modify this value.

- **Scale Grid Snapping and Scale Grid Snap Value:** The Scale Grid Snapping is the final component of the grid snap group. This is useful when attempting to scale things. When the actor is active, it will scale up or down in precise increments that may be selected in the Scale Grid Snap Value option.

- **Camera Speed:** After Scale Grid Snapping, we have Camera Speed. The arrow keys are used to move the camera around. We may control how quickly the camera moves by adjusting its speed in the Camera Speed option.

- **Maximize or Restore Viewport:** The Maximize or Restore Viewport button is the last item on the Viewport toolbar, located in the far right corner. As said before, there are four Viewport kinds to choose from: perspective, front, side, and top. When you click, the Viewport is separated into four segments, one for each Viewport kind. The Side view is at the top left, the Front view is at the top right, the Perspective view is at the bottom left, and the Top view is at the bottom right. Each window has its toolbar for the

Viewport. Any viewport type may be maximized by clicking the Maximize or Restore Viewport button on the Viewport you want to maximize. This viewport option is significant when creating levels and putting objects since we want to ensure correctly aligned from all angles. As a result, be prepared to swap between those settings regularly.

MODES

The Modes pane displays the many modes available in the Editor. We may select the method to use in the Editor from this panel based on the work at hand.

There are five modes to choose from, each represented by a distinct icon.

They are as follows:

- **Place Mode:** This is the standard mode. It's utilized to put actors on your level. An actor is everything you put in your game, such as static meshes, lighting, triggers, volumes, and so on. This is comparable to the usage of entities or objects in other game engines. Many actors may be placed in the level, particularly performers who appear in all types of productions. All of these actors have been classified into classes based on their kind. There are five different sorts of courses. These are their names:

  - **Basic:** This category covers the most basic actors, as well as those that may be found in almost every game you create. Triggers, cameras, player start, and so forth are examples of these.

- **Lights:** The lights panel displays the many sorts of light actors that are available. For example, point lights function similarly to a standard light bulb by producing light evenly from a point source in all directions, and directional lights, which emit light from an indefinitely distant source, such as the sun so on.

- **Visual:** This class includes all of the characters that impact the game's aesthetics, such as post-processing volumes, atmospheric fog, decals, and so on.

- **BSP Brushes:** BSP brushes, also known as Binary Space Partitioning, are the essential building elements for constructing in-game geometry. The class includes BSP brushes in various forms, including the box, cone, spiral staircase, and so on.

- **Volumes:** The volumes class comprises various volumes, each with its own set of properties. For instance, you have the KillZ Volume, which destroys any actor that enters it, even the Player actor. This is important for creating traps and locations where the ground might collapse.

- **Paint Mode:** In Paint Mode, we may paint and modify colors and textures on static models. We may adjust the brush size, falloff radius, strength, and other parameters here. One thing to keep in mind is that we can only paint on the presently chosen actor, ensuring that we only paint on the mesh and not somewhere else.

- **Landscape Mode:** If we have a natural outdoor environment, instead of developing the complete landscape in a 3D modeling software and then importing it into the Engine, we may create it directly in the Engine using the Landscape tool. When the landscape tool is used, a large green plane appears in the viewer. This shows we how big the landscape will be after it's finished.

  If we have a natural outdoor environment, instead of developing the complete landscape in a 3D modeling software and then importing it into the Engine, we may create it directly in the Engine using the Landscape tool. When the landscape tool is used, a large green plane appears in the viewer. This shows we how big the landscape will be after it's finished. In the window, you may change the dimensions and other options. When we're finished, click the Create button at the bottom of the modes window, and the landscape plane will be created. After you've constructed the aircraft, you may sculpt and paint it to make your environment. To erase the aircraft, activate the location mode, pick the plane, and push Delete to remove it.

- **Foliage Mode:** In this mode, you may rapidly paint static meshes on landscape planes and other static meshes using paint selection (place) and erase static meshes. This is a valuable tool for putting objects such as trees, plants, shrubs, rocks, and so on, thus the name Foliage Mode. Instead of planting each tree, rock, and shrub in your level one by one, we may utilize this tool to do it. In the Foliage Mode, we may choose the density of the mesh to be placed, the brush size, and which actor or actors to use.

- **Geometry Editing Mode:** Last but not least, we have the Geometry Editing Mode. As previously stated, BSP brushes are the fundamental building elements for our in-game geometry and are highly helpful. However, the BSP brushes that were supplied to us were of a particular form. If we need a different form for the BSP brush, we may go to the Geometry Editing Mode and then manually edit our BSP brush.

Finally, if we want to discover a particular actor, we can type their name into the search bar at the top, and it will display the actors whose names match the one we entered.

OUTLINER OF THE WORLD

In a hierarchical style, the World Outliner presents all of the actors at your level. The Scene Outliner window allows you to choose and change actors. It's an excellent technique to keep track of which actors are present in the scene. When creating a somewhat huge level, it is typical for developers to neglect to remove certain characters from the scene that they no longer require. As a result, these actors remain in the scene when the game is running and consume unneeded memory. One method to avoid this is to use the World Outliner.

The World Outliner allows you to execute the following operations:

- **Build Folders:** You may create a folder and place actors in it.

  In the above snapshot, for example, there is a folder labeled Lighting that includes all of the light actors present in the scene. This makes it much easier to keep track of your valuables. It also makes everything appear nice, tidy, and organized.

Grouping actors into folders is also valuable when you wish to relocate certain players without disrupting their relative position to one another.

Assume you've created an interior scenario and wish to relocate it to a different place. Instead of relocating or group selecting all of the assets individually, you may group all of the items in the room into a container. If you wish to relocate the room, simply click on the folder, and all of the assets in the room will be chosen, allowing you to move them all at once without affecting their relative positions. To select all of the objects in a folder, right-click on it to bring up a menu. Then, with the mouse above select, click on AllDescendants.

- **Hide Function:** We may have seen an eye-shaped symbol to the left of each actor/folder. This is the function of hiding. When we click on it, the associated actor in the scene will be concealed. If it's a folder, all actors in that folder will be masked.

- **Attach Players:** You have the option of attaching two or more actors. This is an additional and comparatively faster method of relocating a group of actors without disrupting their relative location from one another. To do so, just pick the actor in the Scene Outliner window, drag it over to the actor you want to connect it to, and then release it when you get a popup stating Attach *actor name* to *other actor name*. You may also connect several actors to a single actor.

- **Attaching Forms—A Hierarchical Approach:** The actor to whom we link other actors takes on the role of a parent actor. When we move the parent actor, all of the actors linked to it move with it. However, moving the connected actor does not cause the parent actor to move.

  To bring the linked actors together, we must first pick the parent actor from the Scene Outliner and then move it. Only the parent actor will move if we pick it from the Viewport; the other connected actors would not.

We may see several actors in our scene in the bottom left. View Options is located in the bottom-right corner and allows one to select which actors we wish to watch based on criteria in the View Options menu.

BROWSER OF CONTENTS

The Content Browser displays all of our game assets, such as static models, materials, textures, blueprints, audio files, and so on. It is where our assets are imported, organized, viewed, and created.

There are three icons at the top: Add New, Import, and Save All. The following is a description of them:

- **Add New:** We may use this button to create a new asset, such as a material, particle system, blueprint, and so on.

- **Import:** If we wish to import content into your project file, use the import function.

- **Save All:** If we create or modify an asset in the Content Browser, click Save All to save all modified or generated assets.

The navigation bar is located beneath these symbols. If we have many folders and subfolders in our Content Browser, this will assist us in navigating through them fast. There is a little padlock symbol in the far right corner, which is unlocked by default. If click on it, all find in Content Browser requests will be locked. When we right-click on an actor in the Viewport, a menu appears.

There is a feature within it called Find in Content Browser. When we click on it, the Content Browser displays the location of the object. If the asset is locked, clicking Find in Content Browser will not show us where it is located. Instead, it will launch a new Content Browser window, displaying the actor's location. The Sources Panel is located on the left, beneath the navigation bar.

All of the folders and collections in our project are listed in the Sources Panel. The Asset View, on the right, displays all of the assets and subfolders included within the Sources Panel's selected folder. The Filters menu is located at the top of the page. If we just want to see a specific sort of asset, for example, what material assets are present within the folder we've selected, you may do so using the Filters option. To its right is the Search Bar, which may be used to locate a specific asset within the specified folder.

The total number of objects, including assets and folders within the chosen folder, may be found at the bottom of the Asset View. The View Options menu is located on the bottom right and allows us to customize how the items in the Asset View are displayed. We may, for instance, choose whether to view the items as tiles, a list, or a column.

FEATURES

The attributes of the currently chosen actor can be seen and modified in the Details panels. The name of the selected actor is shown at the top.

This is the name field, where we may change the actor's name to whatever like. The lock button is located on the far right. It is unlocked by default. When the Information panel is locked, it will only show the attributes or details of that actor, even if we have picked a different actor.

Below this is a search box, which you can use to narrow down whatever properties we want to see. The Property Matrix button, which opens the Property Editor window, is located next to it. The Display Filter button is on the far right, and it allows us to do things like collapse/expand all of the categories, only display changed attributes, and show all of the having higher in the Details box.

There are two buttons beneath the name: Add Component and Blueprint/Add Script.

As the name implies, the Add Component command allows you to add a component to the currently chosen actor. Static meshes, form primitives, light actors, and other elements are among them. This is comparable to the World Outliner's Attach Actors feature. The actors are linked hierarchically, with the chosen actor serving as the parent.

You may transform the selected actor into a Blueprint Class in addition to adding components. A Blueprint Class is an actor that element analysis as well as code.

Lastly, in the end, there is the Attributes Area, which shows all of the chosen actor's properties, such as position, spin, scaling, what material is presently on it, inserting and removing materials, and so on which we may change.

CONTROLS AND HOTKEYS

We will conclude the Editor's explanation by identifying specific window controls and hotkeys that we should be familiar with. Remember them. It will make using the Editor easier and more efficient. The following are the critical controls that we should be aware of:

- **Control Action Left-Mouse Button:** This chooses the actor who is currently beneath the cursor.

- **Left-Mouse Button + Mouse Drag:** This turns the camera left and right and moves it forward and backward.

- **Right-Mouse Button:** This picks the actor beneath the cursor and opens the actor's settings menu.

- **Right-Mouse Button + Drag:** This causes the camera to spin in the direction you drag the mouse.

- **Left-Mouse Button + Right Mouse Button + Drag:** Depending on where you move your mouse, this will move the camera up, down, left, and right.

- **Middle-Mouse Button + Drag:** Depending on where you move your mouse, this moves the camera up, down, left, and right.

- **Scroll Up:** This advances the camera ahead.

- **Scroll Down:** This causes the camera to travel backward.

- **F:** This zooms in and concentrates on the actor of choice.

- **Arrow Keys:** This causes the camera to go forward, backward, to the left, and the right.

- **W:** This option is used to pick the translation tool.

- **E:** This activates the rotation tool.

- **R:** This enables the scale tool.

- **W + Any Mouse Button:** This advances the camera ahead.

- **S + Any Mouse Button:** This causes the camera to travel backward.

- **A + Any Mouse Button:** This shifts the camera to the left.

- **D + Any Mouse Button:** This causes the camera to shift to the right.

- **E + Any Mouse Button:** This raises the camera.

- **Q + Any Mouse Button:** This lowers the camera.

- **Z + Any Mouse Button:** This broadens the range of view.

- **C + Any Mouse Button:** This narrows the field of view.

- **Ctrl + S:** This helps to save the scene.

- **Ctrl + N:** This results in the creation of a new scene.

- **Ctrl + O:** This launches a previously stored scene.

- **Ctrl + Alt + S:** This option allows you to save a scene in a different format.

- **Alt + Left-Mouse Button+ Drag:** This duplicates the specified actor.

- **Alt + Left Mouse Button + Drag:** This completes a 360-degree rotation of the camera.

- **Alt + Right-Mouse-Button + Drag:** This causes the camera to travel forward or backward.

- **Alt + P:** This allows you to enter play mode Esc. This disables the play mode.

- **F11:** This activates the immersive mode.

- **G:** This activates the game mode.

CREATING A C++ PROJECT

This Getting Started guide will teach you how to create a C++ project in the Unreal Engine and write your first C++ gameplay class in Visual Studio. By the end of this lesson, you should be able to accomplish the following:

- Set up a new C++ project.

- In C++, create a new Actor class.

- In a programming environment, modify the C++ class by adding visual representation and functionality.

- Compile project.

- In the Unreal Editor, put our new Actor to the test.

This instruction assumes we've already installed Visual Studio as our development environment. If not, please see

Setting Up Visual Studio for the Unreal Engine for information on installing and configuring it for Unreal Engine programming. We also assume that we are familiar with the Unreal Editor before beginning this article. Still, for our convenience, we will walk through all of the processes required to build and manage C++ classes from the editors. The ultimate result of this method will be a cube that hovers softly in mid-air and spins continuously, providing a simple item to evaluate. At the same time, learn to utilize the development environment for programming.

Setup Is Required

Start the Unreal Editor. When the Project Browser appears, pick the Games Project category and a Blank template. Check that C++ and Starter Content is enabled, then select your chosen Save Location and Name for this project and click Create Project. In this case, we're calling our project QuickStart.

This will generate a simple, blank project with only the necessary C++ code in the solution, opening in both the Unreal Editor and Visual Studio.

Make a New Class in C++

1. Click the File drop-down menu in the Unreal Editor and pick the New C++ Class ... option.

2. The Select Parent Class option will appear. We can extend an existing class by adding functionality to your own. Select Actor as the essential item that may be put in the world, then click Next.

3. Name your Actor FloatingActor in the Name Your New Actor option and then click Create Class.

4. With our new class selected in the Content Browser, the Unreal Engine will immediately compile and reload, and our programming environment will open with FloatingActor.cpp.

Changes to Your C++ Class

Now that we've built our C++ Class, we'll open Visual Studio and begin editing our code.

1. Locate the Solution Explorer in Visual Studio, which is by default on the left side of the window, and then use it to locate FloatingActor.h. It will be found in our project under Games > QuickStart > Source > QuickStart.

2. To open and bring FloatingActor.h into focus in the text editor, double-click it. This is an example of a header file. Consider it to be similar to a table of contents for a C++ class. Before we can begin adding new functionality, we must define any new variables or functions used in this file.

3. Add the following code under the AFloatingActor() declaration:

```
UPROPERTY(Visible_Anywhere)
UStaticMeshComponent* Visual_Mesh;
```

In this case, we're declaring a StaticMeshComponent, which will serve as our object's visual representation.

It's worth noting that it employs a UProperty macro, making it visible within the Unreal Editor. More information about UProperty and its specifiers may be found here.

4. Now, open Floating Actor.cpp and paste the following code into AFloatingActor:: AFloatingActor() Before the closing bracket:

```
Visual_Mesh = CreateDefault_Subobject<
UStaticMeshComponent>(TEXT("Mesh"));
Visual_Mesh->SetupAttachment(RootCompo
nent);
static Constructor_Helpers::FObjectFin
der<UStaticMesh> Cube_
VisualAsset(TEXT("/Game/StarterContent/
Shapes/Shape_Cube.Shape_Cube"));

if (Cube_VisualAsset.Succeeded())
{
    Visual_Mesh-
>SetStaticMesh(CubeVisualAsset.Object);
    Visual_Mesh-
>SetRelativeLocation(FVector(0.0f,
0.0f, 0.0f));
}
```

This method is the function constructor, and it instructs the class on how to initialize itself when it is created for the first time. The code we've added will create a new StaticMesh_Component to our Visual_Mesh reference, bind it to our Actor, and set it to the cube mesh from the Starter Content files.

5. Insert the following code within **AFloatingActor:Tick(float DeltaTime) Just before the closing bracket:

```
FVector New_Location =
GetActorLocation();
FRotator New_Rotation =
GetActorRotation();
float Running_Time =
GetGameTimeSinceCreation();
float Delta_Height =
(FMath::Sin(Running_Time + DeltaTime) -
FMath::Sin(Running_Time));
NewLocation.Z += Delta_Height * 20.0f;
float Delta_Rotation = DeltaTime *
20.0f;
New_Rotation.Yaw += DeltaRotation;
SetActorLocationAndRotation(New_
Location, New_Rotation);
```

The Tick function is where we put code that will be executed in real-time. In this example, it will cause our cube to rotate while also bouncing up and down.

Compile and Test C++ Code

1. Save work in FloatingActor.h as well as FloatingActor. cpp. Then, in the Solution Explorer, right-click the project and select the Build command from the context menu. Finally, wait for the project to complete compiling.

The Output log at the bottom of the window should see a message that reads "Success."

Alternatively, we may return to the Unreal Editor and choose Compile from the toolbar at the top of the page.

2. Return to the Unreal Editor's Content Browser, expand C++ Classes, and then look for FloatingActor. It will be placed in the same folder as our project, in our instance, QuickStart.

3. To create an instance of FloatingActor, click and drag it into the Perspective Viewport. It will be chosen as "FloatingActor1" in the World Outliner, and its characteristics will be shown in the Details Panel.

4. Set your Actor's Location in the Details Panel for FloatingActor1 to (−180, 0, 180). In the default scenario, this will position it precisely above the table. We may also manually relocate it, thereby using the Move gizmo.

5. At the top of the screen, press the Play In Editor button.

Final Result

The cube should now be softly floating up and down over the surface as it slowly spins.

Congratulations! We've just finished writing your first Actor class entirely in C++! While this specific object scratches the surface of what we can accomplish with C++ source code, you have now covered all the fundamentals of generating, modifying, and compiling C++ code for your game. We are now prepared to take on more difficult gameplay programming tasks.

- Now that we've learned how to create a basic C++ Actor experiment with making it more customizable. We may, for example, add variables to modify its behavior:

  - **In FloatingActor.h:**

    ```
    public:
        UPROPERTY(EditAnywhere,
    BlueprintReadWrite,
    Category="FloatingActor")
        float Float_Speed = 20.0f;

        UPROPERTY(EditAnywhere,
    BlueprintReadWrite,
    Category="FloatingActor")
        float Rotation_Speed = 20.0f;
    ```

  - **In FloatingActor.cpp:**

    ```
    NewLocation.Z += Delta_Height *
    FloatSpeed;
    float Delta_Rotation = Delta_Time *
    RotationSpeed;
    ```

We can now modify the float and rotation speed in the Details Panel when we pick our Actor by adding these variables in the header and changing the float values we were using to scale Delta_Height and Delta_Rotation in the .cpp.

Experiment with different types of behavior for the Tick function by utilizing Location, Rotation, and Scale.

In C++, we may also attempt attaching additional types of components to make a more complicated entity.

Refer to the Creating and Attaching Components tutorial for examples of the many sorts of features we may use and try adding a Particle System Component to give your floating object some flare.

Finally, if we right-click the Actor class in the Content Browser, we may extend it in C++ or Blueprint, allowing you to build different versions.

We may have an entire library of FloatingActors, each with its own set of Meshes and parameters.

Source Code:

- **FloatingActor.h**

```
#pragma once

#include "CoreMinimal.h"
#include "GameFramework/Actor.h"
#include "FloatingActor.
generated.h"

UCLASS()
class QUICK_START_API AFloatingActor
: public AActor
{
    GENERATED_BODY()

public:
    // Sets default values
    AFloatingActor();

    UPROPERTY(Visible_Anywhere)
    UStaticMeshComponent*
Visual_Mesh;
```

```
protected:
    // Called when game starts
    virtual void BeginPlay()
override;

public:
    // Called frame
    virtual void Tick(float
DeltaTime) override;

};
```

- **FloatingActor.cpp**

```
#include "FloatingActor.h"

// default values Sets
AFloatingActor::AFloatingActor()
{
    // Set this actor to call Tick()
    PrimaryActorTick.bCanEverTick =
true;

    Visual_Mesh = CreateDefault_
Subobject<UStaticMeshComponent>(TEXT
("Mesh"));
    Visual_Mesh->SetupAttachment(Roo
tComponent);

    static Constructor_
Helpers::FObjectFinder<UStaticMesh>
CubeVisualAsset(TEXT("/Game/
StarterContent/Shapes/Shape_Cube.
Shape_Cube"));
```

```
    if (Cube_VisualAsset.
Succeeded())
    {
        VisualMesh-
>SetStaticMesh(CubeVisualAsset.
Object);
        VisualMesh-
>SetRelativeLocation(FVector(0.0f,
0.0f, 0.0f));
    }
}

// Called when game starts
void AFloatingActor::BeginPlay()
{
    Super::BeginPlay();

}

// Called frame
void AFloatingActor::Tick(float
DeltaTime)
{
    Super::Tick(DeltaTime);

    FVector New_Location =
GetActorLocation();
    FRotator New_Rotation =
GetActorRotation();
    float Running_Time =
GetGameTimeSinceCreation();
    float Delta_Height =
(FMath::Sin(Running_Time + Delta_
Time) - FMath::Sin(Running_Time));
```

```
    NewLocation.Z += DeltaHeight *
20.0f;        //Scale our height by a
factor of 20
    float Delta_Rotation = DeltaTime
* 20.0f;     //Rotate by 20 degrees
per second
    New_Rotation.Yaw += DeltaRotation;
    SetActorLocationAndRotation(NewL
ocation, New_Rotation);
}
```

THE FIRST STEPS IN CREATING A GAME

We should have everything set up by now. We've learned enough for us to finally get started with what we're here for making games using UE4.

Because it is so much you can accomplish with this powerful engine, one of the best things about UE4 is that it is simple to learn yet challenging to master. We will begin by creating the game's fundamental elements, including the level, lighting, and materials.

We will discuss the following things in this chapter:

- What is a project, the many types of tasks provided by UE4, loading, and creating new projects.

- The concept, goal, genre, and characteristics of our game.

- Brushes for geometry and BSP.

- Adding assets to the Content Browser and the level.

- How to make materials.

- Lighting, including kinds, applications, and building lighting.

Project

A project is a container for all materials, maps, and code that comprise our game. Once we've established a project, one may add levels or scenes to it.

You can build and utilize our project files that have been created or purchased. Most projects available for purchase are packaged as a theme, complete with materials and levels based on that theme. For example, the Sci-Fi Hallway project is available for free download from the Marketplace. This project file includes various items, materials, and a level layout of a future corridor.

Developing a New Project

When starting a new project, UE4 provides a variety of templates from which to pick based on the sort of game you want to create. Let's take a closer look at Unreal Project Browser to see what I mean:

There are many sorts of templates accessible, as we can see.

These are project files that you may build that include the framework for the game need to produce. For example, suppose you want to develop a third-person shooter or adventure game. In that case, we may select Third Person, which includes programmed elements such as the camera, characters, and basic mechanics. It also includes an example map on which we can test the controls and mechanics. To start a new project, just select the game we want to make and click the Create Project button.

Taking over an Established Project

There are numerous methods for starting a project. One way is to go to My Projects and then to the Engine Launcher

Library area. The second method is to use the Projects panel in the Unreal Project Browser. The third method is to load a project directly from the Editor. To do so, open the File menu by clicking on the File icon in the menu bar, then pick Open Project and choose the project we want to open. The current project will be closed, and the Editor will be reopened as a result.

Structure of the Project's Directory

Any projects we create are saved by default under C:\ Users*account name* Documents\Unreal Projects. When you open this folder:

Each project is housed in its folder. Each folder includes project-related files and directories such as assets, maps, the project file or .uproject files, and so on. Take a peek around to discover which folders contain what and what role they each perform. To delete a project, just delete the folder containing the project you want to delete.

Bloques

We've got our project all set up. We can begin developing our game. Let's start with a definition of the game.

Bloques is a first-person puzzle game created for Android, and it is the game we will make in this guide. The game's primary goal is to solve a series of riddles in each area to go on to the next. The game we're planning to develop will feature four rooms, with the problem becoming more complicated with each progressing level.

Controls

The user controls the character through two virtual joysticks, one for movement and the other for gazing. Touch will be used for every game interaction, such as picking up things, unlocking doors, and so on.

Creating the Game's Project

The first step is to establish a project. Launch the Editor from the Engine Launcher by clicking the Launch button. This game was created using version 4.7.6. After launching the Unreal Project Browser, navigate to the New Project panel and complete the following steps:

1. In the Blueprint tab, pick the template First Person from the templates area.

2. Select Mobile/Tablet from the Target Hardware choices.

3. We have two options in the Quality Settings: Maximum Quality and Scalable 2D or 3D. As previously stated, we should only select Maximum Quality if we create a game for PC or Console and Scalable 2D or 3D if we create a game for mobile or tablet. Select Scalable 2D or 3D with that in mind.

4. Select No Starter Content from the option that asks whether we want to start with or without starter content.

5. Finally, give the project the name Bloques.

Then, simply click on the Create Project button. Our project is now up and running. When you launch the Editor, we'll notice that a test level has already been created. The purpose of the test level is to demonstrate the fundamental functions and mechanics provided by the template you've chosen. The player will be able to move, leap, and shoot in the First Person template. Another wonderful feature is that when we choose Mobile/Tablet as our target hardware, UE4 will automatically give two virtual game-pads, one for moving and viewing. This eliminates the need to script in the controls, which saves time.

We, on the other hand, do not wish to work on this sample map. We'd want to create a new map. To do so, open the File menu and select New Level from the drop-down menu. The New Level box appears when we click on it, with two types of levels available: Default and Empty. A Default Level already has the essential components, such as a sky-box and a player start actor.

Empty Level, on the other hand, as the name implies, has nothing set up.

Choose Empty Level if we want to start fresh with your game. We don't need a skybox because our game will be played indoors. As a result, select Empty Level. We've now created the level on which we'll build our game. Let's call this level Bloques Game for now. Our Viewport should now look something like this:

Brushes for BSP

The first step is to construct our level. This will be accomplished with the assistance of BSP brushes. We discussed BSP brushes briefly in Chapter 2, but today we'll go over them in further depth. BSP brushes are used to build levels' volumes and surfaces. It allows you to quickly and easily block out our level and create rapid prototypes. We may also use BSP brushes to construct the entire level. If we do not have access to 3D modeling tools such as Maya or 3DS Max to generate components for our level (such as walls, ceilings, and so on), we may design your level using

BSP brushes instead. The BSP brushes may be found in the Place Mode in the Modes panel.

Brushes Using Default BSP Forms

UE4 comes with a total of seven preset brushes. From left to right, there are:

- **Box Brush:** Makes a cube-shaped brush. You may customize the box's length, width, and height. You may optionally specify whether the cube should be hollow or not. If this is the case, we have the option of adjusting the thickness of the walls.

- **Sphere Brush:** This tool produces a spherical brush. We have control over the amount of tessellations. Increasing the number of tessellations will smooth it out and make it look more like a real spherical. However, keep in mind that raising the tessellations increases the number of surfaces and hence the amount of memory required to render. Keeping this in mind and the technological constraints of mobile devices, it is preferable to have low-polygon geometry with a decent texture rather than high-polygon geometry with a terrible texture.

- **Cylinder Brush:** A cylindrical brush is created by pressing this button. Its radius and height may be customized. We can also choose to have more or fewer sides. As with the Sphere Brush, increasing the number of sides increases the number of surfaces along the length, rendering it smoother but necessitating more memory to draw.

- **Cone Brush:** Makes a conical brush. You may change characteristics like the height and radius of the base. We may also specify how many surfaces the brush should have.

- **Linear Stair Brush:** This tool allows you to make straight or linear staircases. Instead of modeling, unwrapping, and importing stairs into your level, we may construct them directly in the engine. We may choose the length, breadth, and height of each step, number of stairs, and distance below the first step.

- **Curved Stair Brush:** The Curved Stair Brush may also be used to build curved staircases. You may change the inner radius of the curve and the angle of the curve (the angle of the curve determines how much the stair will bend). You may choose the angle (anywhere from 0 to 360 degrees), the number of steps, and the distance below the first step. Finally, you may specify whether the steps should be counter-clockwise or clockwise.

- **Spiral Stair Brush:** Last but not least, we have the Spiral Stair Brush. The distinction between Spiral and Curved Stairs is that Spiral Stairs may coil around themselves repeatedly but Curved Stairs cannot. We may choose each step's inner radius, breadth, height, and thickness, the number of steps, and the number of steps in a single spiral. Finally, we may specify whether we want the underside and surface of the stairs to be sloping or stepped and whether you want the spiral to run counter-clockwise or clockwise.

The preceding brush types can be utilized to build geometry by using additive or subtractive brush types in the Place/BSP Modes panel.

When we add a brush to your level and utilize it to build geometry, an additive brush will add geometry wherever it is put. Subtractive brush kinds will eliminate the overlapping additive geometry.

Aside from these options, you may also modify the characteristics of each geometric surface, such as rotating, flipping, panning, and scaling the U and V coordinates. When we add materials to them, we may see the results.

Finally, we may utilize brushes to create volumes like blocking, pain-causing, trigger, and so on.

BSP Brush Editing

We want to use BSP brushes to generate geometry, but the form we need isn't one of the seven preset shapes. In such a scenario, you can use the Geometry Edit mode to design our brush. It's on the far right side of the Modes menu.

Click it to enter the Geometry Edit mode.

When we move to the Geometry Edit mode, we can view all geometry's vertices, faces, and edges. We may have also noticed that the vertices have grown in size. We may pick the entire brush, a vertex, a face, or a geometry edge in this mode.

There are various operations available on the modes panel, such as Create, Delete, Flip, and so on. Some of them we can do, while others you can't. What operations we may and cannot do are determined by the selection.

BSP Brushes Are Being Used to Block Out the Rooms

We will now create the setting for our game. Make four rooms and keep them all shut-off, so the player needs to complete the problem in one area before moving on to the next.

The Very First Room

- The first room will be very easy. The room will be a cuboid shape.

   Because here is where the player begins, they will be taught the mechanics of moving, seeing, picking up, and setting things in this area. The player must pick up the critical cube and set it on the pedestal to open the door. The player will also learn the primary goal of each room by completing this essential job.

   So let's start with the floor. We'll be using a Box Brush. Click on Box in the Modes panel under BSP and drag it onto the Viewport to add a Box Brush. Set the brush's size to 2048 × 2048 × 64 in the Details window.

   We want this area to be relatively small because the task is easy, and we also want to minimize excessive wandering because the player may become bored.

- After that, let's start building the walls. We'll create them using a Box BSP brush once more. Set the size to 2048 × 64 × 1024. After you've created one wall, just click and hold the Alt key while moving it to make a copy that can be put on the opposite side of the room.

- Set the measurements for the walls on the opposite side to 64 × 2048 × 1024. As with the other wall, replicate the BSP brush and transfer it to the opposite side of the room.

- Finally, replicate the floor and drag it on top of the walls to create the ceiling. This room now requires a hole for the door. Instead, the player would be trapped in the first area and unable to go to the next. We'll achieve this with the assistance of a subtractive BSP brush.

- To make a subtractive brush, drag the Box Brush onto the level and change the Brush Type to Subtractive in the Details panel. This should be 64 × 256 × 256 in size. Apply this subtractive brush to any of the walls all along the room's smaller side.

- Finally, let's put a pedestal near the door where the player must set the key cube to unlock it.

- With that, we've effectively walled off the first room. Let's get to the next one.

The Second Space

- We'll make the second chamber a little more difficult for the gamer. When you enter the second chamber, there will be a massive door in the center. By tapping the door on the screen, the player can open it. The door, however, closes as soon as they lift their finger or step away from it. The key cube will be to the player's right, but it is imprisoned.

- To open the key cube, the player must proceed past the door, fetch another cube, set it on a platform near the entrance, unlock the key cube, place it on the pedestal, and proceed to the next chamber.

- We had separately built each surface (walls, floor, and ceiling) in the first chamber. We have another option for constructing our second room. In the Details panel of the brush, we'll utilize the Hollow attribute to do this.

- As a result, pick the Box Brush and move it onto the scene. Set its size to 2048 × 1544 × 1024 and place it just next to the first room.

- Once you've got the brush in place, go to the Details panel and check the Hollow box.

- When you click it, a new setting, Wall Thickness, becomes accessible. Set its value to 128 (make sure the subtractive brush we used for the door in the previous room overlaps both walls; otherwise, you won't be able to see the door).

- That's all there is to it! We have our second room boxed out without spending a lot of time installing each piece of furniture and ensuring that they are correctly aligned. Only the pedestals and the aperture for the entrance leading to the third chamber need to be installed. Simply repeat the process we used for the previous room, creating a subtractive brush with dimensions of 64 × 256 × 256 and positioning it on the other side of the room. Similarly, duplicate the subtractive brush for the first room and transfer its copy to the opposite side of the room.

- Finally, in this space, we will add two pedestals to complete the look. One pedestal will be toward the center of the room, near the massive door. To unlock the second key cube, the player must place the first key cube on this pedestal.

- The second pedestal is located on the opposite side of the chamber, and it is here that the player must set the key cube to unlock the door and go to the third room.

- With this, we have completed the blocking out of the second room. Let's continue to the third section, where things start to become interesting.

The Third Space

- By this point, the player should be familiar with the game's fundamental principles and controls. Let us now present them with a more difficult challenge in the third chamber. When the player enters the third chamber, there will be a pit between them and the door to the final room. A bridge will be required for the player to be able to traverse the pit.

- To construct the bridge, the player must lead an artificial intelligence (AI)-controlled item onto a switch. The item will follow a route. Parts of the pieces, however, are missing.

- With the aid of switches placed around the level, the player may fill up the gaps. The difficulty here is deciding which switch to press and when to press it. It also depends on time. After the object has arrived at its location, the bridge will be drawn, allowing the player to cross, take the key cube, unlock the door, and go to the next level.

- There are two ways to build the pit; the first is to divide the room into two halves. The first section would be on one side of the pit, while the second would be on the other.

- After completing the two components, build the pit and finally put them. However, this is a poor and time-consuming method of building the chamber and pit. We'd also have more surfaces, which would need more memory when displaying the level.

- You would also have to meticulously line up all of the pieces to ensure there are no gaps.

- The second method, which we will employ instead, is to construct the entire chamber and then carve out the pit using a subtractive brush. We won't have to worry about different faces aligning different space areas, and we can change the pit's dimensions by moving and modifying the subtractive brush.

- As is customary, we'll start by laying the groundwork. Now that we're going to cut out the pit, the floor will be higher than in the other rooms. Choose the Box Brush and make its dimensions 4096 × 2048 × 512. This will be the primary area where the puzzle will be located.

- Because this chamber is higher than the previous ones, we'll need some steps to get the player to the third room. First, add a tiny Box Brush with the dimensions 512 × 1544 × 64 and position it near the previous room's entrance.

- Drag the Linear Stair Brush from the Modes panel onto the level to build the stairs.

- Set the stair width to 1544 and the number of steps to 23. Position the stairs near the edge of the Box Brush we previously built; finally, take the floor from the third chamber and place it next to the stairs.

- We'll need a Box subtractive brush to add the pit. Another method for picking a subtractive brush is choosing the brush shape, which in this example is the Box Brush, and then, at the bottom of the Modes panel, change the brush type to additive or subtractive. Simply choose subtractively and drag the brush over the level.

- We must ensure that the hole is large enough that the player cannot leap across it and deep enough that the player cannot skip out if they fall into it. Keeping this in mind, make the brush's dimensions 640 × 2304 × 512. Place the pit at the other end of the room.

- We now need to put up the walls. In a few phases, we will build walls to this space. First, choose a Box brush, set its size to 4096 × 64 × 512, and put it along the room's longest side. Duplicate the first wall and place it on the opposite side.

- Next, we'll build some walls along the stairs and passageways leading to the third chamber. Set the measurements to 1202 × 64 × 1024 and position those on either side of the steps, making sure they all line up perfectly and there are no gaps between the brushes.

- We may have noticed a gap between the walls of the corridor and the walls along the longer side of the chamber. Let's fill in the gaps with a $64 \times 188 \times 512$ Box brush. Fill in the spaces with two of them, one on each side.

- Finally, the wall we'll build is on the far side of the room, along the shorter side. Set the Box Brush size to $64 \times 2048 \times 512$, put the final wall using a subtractive brush for the entrance.

- We need to add a few more items to the room now that we've blacked it out before moving to the fourth and final room. First, we'll put up some panels with switches on them that the player may use to steer the object across the pit. To make the panels, simply replicate the pedestals from the previous rooms and set them in this one. Place them near either of the longer walls and make sure the player can see the opposite wall.

- Finally, position a pedestal at the front entrance. With this, we have completed the blocking out of the third chamber. Let's now close off the fourth and last room.

The Fourth Space

- We simply need to block out one more room. We had different problems and objectives in each of the prior three rooms. We'll merge all of the riddles from the previous room in the fourth room. The player's task in this room is identical to that of the last room: guide an AI-controlled item through obstacles such as doors and pits to the other side of the area. The item will follow a specified route until it reaches its destination. If it collides with a door or falls into a pit, it returns to its initial location.

- Because we will have pits, the room's height will be identical to the prior ones. This will also be the most significant room. Keeping this in mind, we'll create the floor by using a Box Brush with dimensions of 5120 × 2048 × 512.

- We're going to dig some trenches now that we have the floor. Create a Box brush using the subtractive mode again, this time with dimensions 728 × 1928 × 512, and put it near the entrance. We'll have three pits in this chamber, so duplicate the subtractive brush by holding down the Alt key, making two duplicates, and put them throughout the map.

- Then there's the wall. Simply replicate the walls from the third room on the longer side. Set the value of X to 5120 in the Details window, and then just position the wall.

  Duplicate and position the second wall. You may do the same for the shorter side—replicate and position the shorter sidewall (the one with the door) at the other end of the room.

- Copy the brush, adjust the Z value to 64, and drag it upward to make the roof.

- Finally, we will put a couple pedestals where the switches will reside.

- With that, we've finished blocking out our final room!

  Now that we've delineated our rooms, let's add some assets make some materials and apply them to our level.

Browser of Contents

When we discussed the Editor's user interface in the previous chapter, we mentioned Content Browser briefly. Let's go through it a little more in-depth. The Content Browser is where all of your project's assets are saved and viewed. Meshes, Map Files, Textures, Skeletal Meshes, Materials, Blueprints, Audio Files, and so on are examples of assets.

There are three icons at the top: Add New, Import, and Save All. The following is a description of them:

- **Add New:** We may use this button to create a new asset, such as a material, particle system, blueprint, and so on.

- **Import:** If we wish to import content into our project file, use the import function.

- **Save All:** If we create or modify an asset in the Content Browser, click Store All to save all modified or generated assets.

The navigation bar is located beneath these symbols. If we have many folders and subfolders in your Content Browser, this will assist you in navigating through them fast. There is a little padlock symbol in the far right corner, which is unlocked by default. If we click on it, all Find in Content Browser requests will be locked. When right-clicking on an actor in the Viewport, a menu appears.

There is a feature within it called Find in Content Browser. When a user clicks on it, the content browser displays the location of the object.

If the asset is locked, clicking Find in Content Browser will not show you where it is located. Instead, it will launch a new Content Browser window, displaying the actor's location.

The Sources Panel is located on the left, beneath the navigation bar. All of the folders and collections in your project are listed in the Sources Panel. The Asset View, on the right, displays all of the assets and subfolders included within the Sources Panel's selected folder. The Filters menu is located at the top of the page.

If we just want to see a specific sort of asset, for example, what material assets are present within the folder we've selected, you may do so using the Filters option. To its right is the Search Bar, which may be used to locate a specific asset within the specified folder.

The total number of objects, including assets and folders within the chosen folder, may be found at the bottom of the Asset View. The View Options menu is located on the bottom right and allows you to customize how the items in the Asset View are displayed. We may, for example, choose whether to view the items as tiles, a list, or columns.

Details

The attributes of the currently chosen actor can be seen and modified in the Details panels. The name of the chosen actor is shown at the top (which, in this case, is Cube06).

This is the name field, where you may change the actor's name to whatever we like.

The lock button is located on the far right. It is unlocked by default. When the Information panel is locked, it will only show the attributes or details of that actor, even if we have picked a different actor.

Below this is a search box, which we can use to narrow down whatever properties you want to see. The Property Matrix button, which opens the Property Editor window, is located next to it. The Display Filter button is on the far right, and it allows you to do things like collapse/expand all of the categories, only display changed attributes, and show all of the advanced properties in the Details box.

There are two buttons beneath the name: Add Component and Blueprint/Add Script.

As the name implies, the Add Component command allows us to add a component to the currently chosen actor. Static meshes form primitives (cube, sphere, cylinder, and cone), light actors, and other elements. This is comparable to the World Outliner's Attach Actors feature. The actors are linked hierarchically, with the chosen actor serving as the parent.

You may transform the selected actor into a Blueprint Class in addition to adding components. A Blueprint Class is an actor that contains components as well as code. (The similar phrase in other engines is Prefab.) In Chapters 3 and 4, we will go through this in great depth.

Finally, at the bottom, there is the Attributes Area, which displays all of the selected actor's properties, such as position, rotation, and scale, what material is presently on it, adding and deleting materials, and so on, which we may change.

Controls and Hotkeys

We will conclude the Editor's explanation by identifying specific window controls and hotkeys that we should be familiar with. Remember them. It will make using the

Editor easier and more efficient. The following are the critical controls that we should be aware of:

- **Left-Mouse Button:** This chooses the actor who is currently beneath the cursor.

- **Left-Mouse Button + Mouse Drag:** This turns the camera left and right and moves it forward and backward.

- **Right-Mouse Button:** This picks the actor beneath the cursor and opens the actor's settings menu.

- **Right-Mouse Button + Drag:** This causes the camera to spin in the direction you drag the mouse.

- **Left-Mouse Button + Right Mouse Button+ Drag:** Depending on where you move your mouse, this will move the camera up, down, left, and right.

- **Middle-Mouse Button + Drag:** Depending on where you move your mouse, this will move the camera up, down, left, and right.

- **Scroll Up:** This pushes the camera.

- **Scroll Down:** This pushes the camera.

- **F:** This zooms in and concentrates on the actor of choice.

- **Arrow Keys:** This causes the camera to go forward, backward, to the left, and the right.

- **W:** This option is used to pick the translation tool.

- **E:** This activates the rotation tool.

- **R:** This activates the scale tool.

- **W + Any Mouse Button:** This shifts the camera.

- **S + Any Mouse Button:** This causes the camera to travel backward.

- **A + Any Mouse Button:** This shifts the camera to the left.

- **D + Any Mouse Button:** This causes the camera to shift to the right.

- **E + Any Mouse Button:** This raises the camera.

- **Q + Any Mouse Button:** This lowers the camera.

- **Z + Any Mouse Button:** This expands the field of view.

- **C + Any Mouse Button:** This narrows the field of view.

- **Ctrl + S:** This helps to save the scenario.

- **Ctrl + N:** This results in the creation of a new scene.

- **Ctrl + O:** This brings up a previously-stored scenario.

- **Ctrl + Alt + S:** This option allows you to save a scene in a different format.

- **Alt + Left-Mouse Button+ Drag:** This duplicates the actor you've chosen.

- **Alt + Left Mouse Button + Drag:** This completes a 360-degree rotation of the camera.

- **Alt + Right-Mouse-Button + Drag:** This causes the camera to travel forward or backward.

- **Alt + P:** This allows you to enter play mode.

- **Esc (While Playing):** This causes the game mode to exit.

- **F11:** This activates immersive mode.

- **G:** This activates game mode.

IN VISUAL STUDIO, INSTALL THE UNREAL ENGINE

C++ with Blueprints, Unreal Engine's visual programming framework, may create Unreal Engine games. When utilizing C++ for Unreal programming, Visual Studio functions as a robust code editor and debugger.

Getting Established

From Visual Studio, open the New Project window by selecting File New Project and navigating to the installed templates, including a Game folder. Inside, you'll see the choices for developing a game that Visual Studio presently offers, which now incorporates Unreal Engine. If you already have Unreal Engine installed on your system, the Unreal Engine template will not show.

We will be taken through a series of dialogues that will assist you through the Unreal Engine installation process by selecting this template.

The Visual Studio installer will begin with the Unreal Engine checked once we pick install. When we click the Next button, we will be presented with a link to the Unreal Engine license, where selecting Update confirms that we have read and agreed on the conditions and proceeds with the installation.

After completing the first Visual Studio installation, the Epic Games Launcher will launch, allowing you to obtain and install the actual Unreal Engine. We must either create an Epic Games account or sign in with an existing one to install Unreal. After logging in, selecting the Install Engine button in the top left corner of the launcher will begin installing the most recent release version of Unreal.

Building an Unreal Project

From the Unreal editor, you may create a new project using Blueprints or C++ code. When you create a C++ project, a Visual Studio solution is immediately produced. It should be noted that this is the preferred method of developing Unreal C++ code because it handles all of the build requirements inside Visual Studio for us.

Opening the Project in Visual Studio

The Unreal editor uses the File > Open Visual Studio menu commands to open the project in VS.

This will open Visual Studio with two tasks: one for the Unreal engine code called and one for our game project code-named the same as our Unreal project. We may now use Visual Studio to edit, create, and debug your Unreal game.

Game Code Management

C++ Class Wizard for Adding Code to Projects

The C++ Class Wizard allows us to quickly and easily add native C++ code classes to our project, which we can then expand with our functionality if desired. This will turn a content-only project into a code project. We may go to the C++ Class Wizard by doing the following:

1. Select File > New C++ Class in the main editor.

2. The C++ Class Wizard will popup, displaying frequently used classes. If we don't find the class you're searching for, we'll need to browse the whole Class hierarchy listing. In the upper-right corner of the window, choose the Show All Classes checkbox. Select the Class you want to add and then click the Next > button.

3. You will then be requested to give your new Class a name. Do so, and then press the Create Class button. The header (.h) and source (.cpp) files will be generated due to this.

4. The code will be opened in Visual Studio and available for modification right away.

Application Framework

Code files may be produced in Visual Studio and added to the game project in the usual way using the Solution Explorer. We may also add code files to the relevant directories outside Visual Studio to automatically rebuild the solution and project files. This makes it simple to add a large number of files fast using the operating system's UI, and it also makes working in teams easier because solution and project files do not need to be synchronized across team members. Each individual only has to sync the code files and recreate the project files locally.

Project Launching in the Development Environment

If we already have your project open in the editor, we can quickly open it in Visual Studio by choosing Open Visual Studio from the File menu.

We may also open the project in Visual Studio using Windows Explorer or the File > Open > Project menu option.

Open the [ProjectName].sln Visual Studio solution from the project's root directory.

Making Project Files

- **.uproject files**

    - Go to the [ProjectName].uproject folder in Windows Explorer.

    - Choose to Generate Visual Studio Files from the context menu when you right-click on the [ProjectName].uproject file.

    - UnrealBuildTool makes changes to the project files and the solution, as well as generates IntelliSense data.

    - To view the game project in Visual Studio, open the [ProjectName].sln Visual Studio solution found in the project's root directory.

Installing Visual Studio for Unreal Engine

Before you begin creating unreal engine-to-visual studio workflow

The table below shows which versions of VS are compatible with the binary version of UE.

A Version of Unreal Engine	The Version of Visual Studio
4.25 or Later	VS 2019 (Default)
4.22 or Later	VS 2017/VS 2019
4.15 or Later	VS 2017
4.10 to 4.14	VS 2015
4.2 to 4.9	VS 2013

The Unreal Engine Prerequisite Installer Run When we install UE via the Epic Launcher or clone it from GitHub, the UE requirement installer is launched immediately. If we install or sync UE from Perforce, we must execute the necessary installer before executing any UE tools you have developed locally. This installer may be found in the source base under [UERootLocation]\Engine\Extras\Redisten-us].

Alternatives for a Fresh Visual Studio Installation   If we are installing VS for the first time, make sure that the following settings are enabled.

C++ Tools: To add C++ tools to our VS installation, make sure to choose Game development using C++ and these extra choices under Workloads.

- Profiling tools for C++.

- AddressSanitizer in C++ (optional).

- SDK for Windows 10 (10.0.18362 or Newer).

Include the UE Installer

To include the UE installation while installing VS, locate the Summary sidebar on the right, open Game Development using C++, and tick the Unreal Engine installer checkbox under Optional.

CONTENT BROWER

The Content Browser is the main section of the Unreal Editor where you may create, import, organize, browse, and change content assets. It also allows you to manage content folders and conduct other essential asset actions, including renaming, moving, copying, and viewing references. All assets in the game may be found and interacted with using the Content Browser.

We may do the following in the Content Browser:

- Navigate to and interact with all of the game's assets.

- Locate assets, whether saved or not:

  - **Text Filter:** Type text in the Search Assets box to search assets by Name, Path, Tags, or Type. By prefixing a search token with a "-," we may exclude assets from our search.

  - **Filter by Asset Type and Other Criteria:** Click the Filters button to filter by asset type and other criteria.

- Organize assets without ever having to pull them from source control:

  - Make Local or Private Collections and save assets in them for later use.

- To share exciting items with our coworkers, create Shared Collections.

- Obtain development aid:

  - Display assets that may have issues.

- Use the Migrate tool to automatically migrate assets and all their dependent assets to different content directories.

Using the Content Browser

The Content Browser may be accessed via the Window menu. We can run up to four instances of the Content Browser at the same time. This is beneficial in several ways, including:

- Various asset categories can be filtered in different Content Browsers, such as one that only displays Static Meshes and another that only displays Materials.

- Moving assets between various directories when we want to view what else is in the folders.

The Content Browser is docked in the lower-left corner of the main Level Editor interface by default, but it may be moved to any location inside the Level Editor or floated as its window.

ASSETS

An Asset is a document for an Unreal Engine project that is represented as a serialized UObject to a file. We may view the Asset Tree by pressing the Show/Hide Sources and Collections button in the Content Browser's Sources Panel.

- The Asset Tree shows a list of folders in your content directories that contain .uasset files.

- When we click on a folder in the Asset Tree, it displays all of the Assets included within that folder and its subfolders.

- When we right-click on a folder, you'll get a list of activities we may take with that folder and its subfolders. This context menu allows us to add new directories to the Asset Tree.

Naming an Asset

When importing or creating an Asset, the user names it. The Asset's route is directly related to the Asset's disc location. This path is automatically defined by the folder in which the Asset is generated or imported. A path of Content/Characters/MyCharacter, for example, would save to/UE4/MyProject/Content/Characters/MyCharacter. MyCharacter.uasset.

Asset Renaming and Transfer

An Asset may be renamed in the Editor by choosing it in the Content Browser and then left-clicking or hitting the F2 key on its name. By selecting and dragging assets in the Content Browser, they may be relocated or transferred to various directories. When an Asset is renamed or relocated in this manner, other Assets that refer to the renamed or moved Asset are correctly updated. An invisible Redirector is left in place of the original Asset. Cleaning up redirectors is as simple as right-clicking in the Content Browser and choosing to Fix Up Redirectors in Folder.

All Assets that referenced a Redirector will point to the Asset at its new location, after which the Redirector will be removed. It is critical to remember that we must resave the Assets. We may delete Assets from the Content Browser by choosing the Asset and clicking the Delete key or using the option in the context menu on the Asset. If another Asset refers to a deleted Asset, a choice appears asking which extant Asset should be used in lieu of the removed one.

The Fix-Up Redirectors in Folder option is available by right-clicking on a folder or anyplace in the Content Browser's Sources Panel.

Management of Asset

Unreal Engine typically loads and unloads Assets automatically. However, in some situations, taking more direct control of the process can result in substantial speed gains, such as reducing or eliminating redundant load times and eliminating hitches during gaming. See the Asset Management page for more information on managing asset loading and unloading. Assets are "boiled" (translated to final, binary forms depending on the Asset type and target platform) and can be split into multiple .pak files for distribution when a project is deployed.

Reducing Source Control Contingency

When a process comprises package files, each of which contains several Assets, source-control conflict might arise. A methodology that instead promotes and supports the creation of numerous distinct Asset files implies that each Asset may be checked out separately. This eliminates source-control contention and workflow constraints.

Furthermore, because a modification to a single Asset requires just one file update, sync time in content management systems is faster with individual Asset files than with packages containing many Assets.

Assets in Unreal Editor are saved in.uasset files, which generally contain only one Asset. Each Asset reference includes a directory-style path that identifies any Asset in the game.

The Content Browser is where assets are produced (or imported). See Working with Content for more information on generating Assets. See the Content Browser for more details on how to use it.

Copying Assets to Other Projects

In the Content Browser, use the Migrate Tool to copy an Asset (and any dependent Assets) for use in another project.

Packs of Asset

If we downloaded Asset packs from the Launcher, we might add the entire contents of the pack to our project (whether open or closed) without opening it or migrating particular Assets.

To include an Asset pack in your project, follow these steps:

- Locate the Asset pack in our Vault, which is at the bottom of the Library tab.

- Click the Add to Project button.

- Choose our project from the list that displays.

- Click the Add to Project button.

All of the content will be contained within a folder named after the Asset pack was installed.

CHAPTER 3

Using Blueprints

Unreal Engine is a gaming engine that is available to both experienced game creators and newcomers. When developing a sophisticated and large-scale game, you'd almost certainly leverage Unreal's built-in C++ support to get complete control over the engine's systems. However, programming might appear to be a complex undertaking for newcomers, especially if they need to master the engine. This is where blueprints come in. A blueprint is the visual scripting mechanism used by Unreal Engine.

WHAT EXACTLY IS VISUAL SCRIPTING?

Visual scripting allows us to construct a logic for your game in a visual format, similar to programming. Blueprints in Unreal are made up of nodes that are linked together. These nodes can be events (for example, whenever we touch the space bar), actions (for example, move the character here), conditions (for example, is this equal to this?), and so on.

DOI: 10.1201/9781003214731-3 **87**

Nodes can have both inputs and outputs. We provide some input values to a node; it calculates what it needs and then returns some outputs for us to utilize.

Flow control is an essential topic in designs. The code is read from the top down in programming, calculating everything along the way. It's the same with blueprints, albeit we may direct the flow's growth. For the flow to pass through, nodes might have an input, an output, or both. You can see several distinct nodes connected by white lines in the figure below. These white lines direct the flow and instruct the compiler on which nodes to activate next. Consider this to be energy, with the white wires energizing nodes along its journey.

Some nodes also have these colored connections on the left and right. These are the values for the input and output. Nodes, such as the DestroyActor node, can accept data to utilize. This node agrees with a Target and destroys it. Some nodes contain inputs as well as outputs. It takes specific values, calculates something with them, and then prints the result.

We may connect several of these nodes and create loops, functions, and events exactly as we would in a programming language.

Here's another illustration of a blueprint. When we push the space bar (which activates the Space Bar node), we raise ourselves into the air. The Delay node will then hold the flow for one second before moving us back down.

There are various online resources available to help us to learn Unreal Engine and the blueprint system. provides their developers with a variety of documents and video lessons to help them master the engine.

PROGRAMMING VS. BLUEPRINTS

We have the option of using blueprints or C++ programming in Unreal, but which should you use? Blueprints may be an excellent method to get into game creation without learning to program when first getting started with the engine. However, if we ever want to make a more complex/large-scale game or work in the business, learning the program may be the next.

If we want to make something in Unreal, it's most certainly possible to do it with blueprints. Player controls, AI opponents, vehicles, and so on. The blueprint system is highly sophisticated, with a vast number of nodes available for use. What we can build is limited by what we don't know; therefore, we encourage just playing with the engine and making some of our plans. Looking at the template projects that come with Unreal is a beautiful way to get started. There are several games, each with its unique system—all developed with blueprints.

BLUEPRINTS INTRODUCTION

The Blueprint Visual Scripting system in Unreal Engine is a comprehensive gameplay scripting system built on creating gameplay pieces from within Unreal Editor utilizing a node-based interface. It defines object-oriented classes or objects in the engine, just like many other common scripting languages. When using UE4, we'll notice that objects defined with Blueprint are frequently referred to simply as "Blueprints."

This approach is versatile and powerful because it allows designers to practically utilize the whole spectrum of concepts and techniques previously exclusively available to programmers. Furthermore, Blueprint-specific markup accessible in Unreal Engine's C++ implementation enables programmers to construct baseline systems that designers may enhance.

How Do Blueprints Function?

Blueprints, in their most basic form, are visually programmed additions to your game. It is possible to construct sophisticated gameplay components by linking Nodes, Events, Functions, and Variables using Wires.

Blueprints define behavior and other functionality by utilizing graphs of Nodes for multiple reasons—object building, particular methods, and general gameplay events—unique to each Blueprint instance.

Blueprint Types Most Commonly Used

Level Blueprints and Blueprint Classes are the most common Blueprint types we will encounter.

- **Blueprint for Levels:** The Level Blueprint performs the same function and has the same features as Kismet in Unreal Engine 3. Each level has its Level Blueprint, which may reference and modify Actors inside the level, control cinematics using Matinee Actors, and handle level-related features such as level streaming, checkpoints, and so on. The Level Blueprint can also interact with Blueprint Classes (examples are provided in the next section) placed in the level, such as reading/setting any variables or triggering any custom events they may contain.

- **Class for Blueprint:** Blueprint Classes are great for creating interactive elements like doors, switches, collectibles, and destructible scenery. The button and the set of doors are independent Blueprints that include the required logic to respond to player overlap events, animate, play sound effects, and alter their materials (the button lights up when pressed, for example).

In this example, hitting the button triggers an event within the door Blueprint, forcing it to open—however, the doors may very well be started by another sort of Blueprint or a Level Blueprint sequence. Because of their self-contained nature, blueprints may be built to be dropped into a level and operate, with minimum preparation necessary. This also implies that changing a Blueprint used throughout a project will update all instances of it.

What Else Can Blueprints Be Used for?

We've spoken about Level Blueprints and Blueprint Classes, and here are a few instances of what the Blueprint system can do.

- **Using Construction Scripts, we may create customizable prefabs:** The Construction Script is a graph inside Blueprint Classes that runs when an Actor is inserted or modified in the editor but not during gameplay. It helps make readily configurable props that help environment artists work quicker, such as a light fixture that automatically adjusts its material to match the color and brightness of its point light component or a Blueprint that randomly spreads foliage meshes across an area.

The Construction Script in the Blueprint generates and organizes the different Static Meshes and lights based on the settings presented in the Blueprint's Details panel. We were able to drop in the demo room Blueprint, specify values for the length, height, and several rooms created (along with a few other variables), and have a complete set of rooms available in minutes with each Content Example map we built.

A Blueprint like this might take some effort to construct at first, but if we know we'll use it frequently, the time saved while building a level and the convenience of making modifications can make it well worth your time.

Make a Playable Video Game Character

Pawns are also a sort of Blueprint Class, and you can use the Blueprint graph to assemble all of the components into a playable character. We may change the camera's behavior, configure input events for the mouse, controller, and touch screens, and build an Animation Blueprint asset to handle skeletal mesh animations.

When we build a new Character Blueprint, it has a character component with much of the functionality required for moving about, leaping, swimming, and falling built-in. All required is to add some input events based on how we want our character to be handled.

Make a HUD

Blueprint script may also be used to build a game's HUD. It is similar to Blueprint Classes in that it can include event sequences and variables. Still, it is assigned to our project's GameMode asset rather than added directly to a level.

We may configure a HUD to read variables from other Blueprints and utilize them to display a health bar, update a score number, or display objective markers, among other things. The HUD may also be used to create hit-boxes for components such as buttons that can be clicked on or can react to touch input in mobile games.

Graphs and Blueprint Editors

Blueprint Elements built in a Blueprint Editor will be used when creating a Level Blueprint or a Blueprint Class. Depending on the sort of Blueprint you are working with, several varieties of Blueprint Editor are accessible. The Graph mode, with its central Graph tab for building out our Blueprint's network, is the primary element of most Blueprint Editors.

DEVELOPING BLUEPRINT CLASSES

Blueprint Assets can be created using any techniques mentioned through the Content Browser or the Level Editor.

Blueprint Asset Creation in the Content Browser

The Content Browser has a dedicated Add New button for generating new Blueprint Assets in the current directory. We may also build a Blueprint Asset at the chosen place by right-clicking in the Asset View or the Asset Tree.

Making Use of the Add New Button

- Click the Add New button in the Content Browser.

- Blueprint Class should be selected from the Create Basic Asset portion of the dropdown menu.

- For our Blueprint Asset, select a Parent Class. For additional information, see Parent Classes.

Making Use of the Asset View

- To bring up the context menu, right-click in the Content Browser's Asset View (right-hand panel).

- Under the Create Basic Asset section, select Blueprint Class.

- For our Blueprint, select a Parent Class.

Making Use of the Asset Tree

- Right-click a folder in the Content Browser's Asset Tree (left-hand panel).

- Select New Asset from the context menu that opens, then Blueprint Class.

- For our Blueprint, select a Parent Class.

In the Level Editor, we may create new levels.

In the Level Editor, we may generate a Blueprint Asset from one or more chosen Actors. The Blueprint we develop will include your Actor (or Actors), as well as any property modifications we make to them in the Level Editor, as well as their spatial connections to one another. This functionality allows us to store multi-Actor systems as a single, reusable Asset.

- In the Level Editor viewport, choose the Actor or Actors.

- Click the Blueprints dropdown menu in the Level Editor toolbar and select Convert Selection to Blueprint Class.

- At this point, the editor will provide us with three ways to make a new Blueprint Asset from the selected Actor or Actors: New Subclass, Child Actors, and Harvest Parts.

- After you've decided on a method, choose the parent Actor class for our new Blueprint Asset from the list at the bottom of the window. If we use the New Subclass method, the parent class will be restricted to the specified Actor's class or its subclasses.

- Our new Blueprint Asset will display in the Content Browser once we've picked a method and a parent class.

New Subclass

This option is only accessible if we have just one Actor chosen. This function generates a Blueprint Asset as a subclass of your Actor or any of its subclasses, integrating whatever modifications we made to the Actor's attributes. This is the most fundamental technique. The Blueprint Asset will preserve any changes we make to the characteristics of the chosen Actor.

Child Actors

The Child Actors function generates a Blueprint Asset based on any Actor class. In the Level Editor viewport, the new Actor will have its default Components and one additional Child Actor Component for each selected Actor. These Child Actor Components will preserve the modifications we've made to the attributes of the chosen Actors.

Components of Harvest

The Harvest Components function generates a single Blueprint Asset based on any Actor class, then harvests and connects the Components of all the selected Actors to the new Actor. Use this approach when our Actors are mainly used as containers for their Components. Numerous Static Mesh Actors, for example, can be effectively combined into a single Actor with multiple Static Mesh Components because they generally display no actions other than rendering and potential collision. However, because AI-controlled characters have Actor-level autonomy in their activities and may require individual management of Components and access to Component data, they must typically stay as separate Actors.

In the Class Viewer, create a new class.

Blueprint Assets may also be created using the Class Viewer. When using the Class Viewer, we may use the following filters to narrow down the shown classes:

- Select Filters from the Class Viewer toolbar.

- Select Blueprint Bases only from the Filters menu.

To build a new Blueprint Asset, go to the class we want to utilize as a foundation. CameraActor is our foundation class in this example.

- Click the menu to the right of the base class we want to use, or right-click on the class itself.

- A context menu will appear with the option Create Blueprint. Click here to launch the Blueprint creation dialogue.

- Enter a name for our Blueprint Asset and choose a location for it to be saved.

- At the top of the Blueprint creation dialogue, click "Create [Path]/[Name]." This will generate our Blueprint Asset and launch the Blueprint Editor.

- Save our new Blueprint Asset to finish the procedure. Click Save in the Blueprint Editor Toolbar to do so.

Placing Nodes
Drag and Drop

The first technique involves dragging and dropping nodes from the MyBlueprint window onto your graph. For example, there are many variables into which we can drag and drop the PlayerHealth variable to utilize in our script.

When we left-click and drag a variable into the Graph window, we are given two options: Get or Set. Selecting Get will produce a Getter node that will get the variable or its value, but selecting Modify will build a Setter node that will enable to set the variable's value. Depending on the type of node, Get may be the only option available in some cases.

The node at the top is a Getter, whereas the node at the bottom is a Setter. For example, the Getter may be used as a requirement for elements in our games (such as getting the Player Health and checking if that value is above a specified range and, if not, killing the player). In the preceding example, the Setter may raise the Player's Health since we are instructing the Player Health variable what its value should be by setting it.

In the same way, we may drag any Functions or Macros we've built into our graph.

When dragging in an Event Dispatcher, several unique context actions become accessible.

When dragging an Event Dispatcher, we may choose the action we want to do from the display context menu.

Search by Context Menu

- The Context Menu, which Right-clicking inside a Blueprint graph can access, will be used most of the time when inserting nodes.

- We may expand any category (or subcategory) from the menu and pick the node to add to the graph.

- There is also a Context-Sensitive option in the top right corner of the window that is enabled by default but can be deactivated and automatically filters the options shown in the menu based on the current context.

- When we right-click and search for Animation with Context-Sensitive turned on, we'll see a filtered list.

- If we uncheck Context-Sensitive and search for Animation, we will see anything connected to animation.

- While right-clicking in the graph brings up the Context Menu, we can also reach the Context Menu by dragging off an existing node.

- We have a Character Movement Component Reference above, and we can add nodes that contextually make sense and are related to the node we are taking off by dragging off its out pin.

- We may change the Max Walk Speed of the character by searching for Set Max Walk and then selecting Set Max Walk Speed from the menu.

Nodes That Are Collapsing

The most straightforward technique of collapsing is Collapsing Nodes into a Linked Graph. These are mainly used for organizing and keeping our Event Graph looking clean and tidy.

- Locate the nodes we wish to collapse on the Blueprint's Graph. We have several nodes in this area that diminish the player's energy when they jump.

- By left-clicking and dragging over the nodes we want to collapse, we may select all of them. Control + Left-click may also be used to add/remove nodes from our selection.

- Once we've selected the nodes, we want to collapse, right-click on any of them, and choose Collapse Nodes.

- The nodes will be compressed into a single Collapsed Graph node, to which we may give a name afterward.

- When we hover your cursor over the Collapsed Graph node, a preview window of the node network appears.

- Double-clicking on the Collapsed Graph will open a new graph with the nodes we've chosen.

- We can add pins to the Inputs and Outputs nodes inside the Collapsed Graph from the Details panel. Execute is inserted by default; here, we have added two Execute Out Pins: OutOfEnergy and CanJump.

  We also changed the graph such that it checks to see whether the player is out of energy before deducting it from the player's total energy.

- To restore the nodes to their original state, right-click on the collapsed node and select Expand Node.

Collapsing to Function

Another approach for collapsing your nodes is to collapse them to a Function. The advantage of collapsing your nodes to a Function rather than a Collapsed Graph is that we may not only call the Function in another part of the script depending on whatever parameters you give, but we can also call the Function from inside a separate Blueprint (as long as we provide a reference to the Blueprint that contains the Function wish to call).

The steps to collapse our nodes to a Function are as follows:

- Right-click on a node with the nodes we wish to collapse selected and select Collapse to Function.

- A new Function will be generated, which we may rename by hitting F2 in the MyBlueprint box when we build our Blueprint, the WARNING! The warning will be removed.

- When we double-click the Function, it will open in a new graph window. Like Collapsed Graphs, we can use the Details panel to add pins to the Inputs and Outputs nodes.

- We can invoke the Function by its name or by any condition we choose. When the letter F is pressed, the Remove Energy Function is invoked.

- We may undo this collapse by right-clicking the Function and choosing the Expand Node option.

Macro Collapsing

We may collapse nodes to a Macro in addition to collapsing to a Collapsed Graph or Function. The easiest way to conceive of a Macro is that it allows us to combine multiple linked nodes into a single node that accomplishes all we need it to do all at once. It is especially beneficial for anything that we regularly perform, such as a complicated math equation.

Steps for compressing nodes to a Macro are provided below:

- Right-click on a node with the nodes we want to collapse selected and select Collapse to Macro.

- A new Macro node will be generated, which we may rename by hitting F2 in the MyBlueprint window.

- Double-clicking on the Macro will launch it. We may add Input or Output pins as needed, just like with the other way of compressing nodes. Here is our Event Graph with the additional pins that implement the Macro.

- We may restore the collapsing of the nodes by right-clicking on our Macro and selecting Expand Node.

OVERVIEW OF THE BLUEPRINT

The Blueprint Visual Scripting system in Unreal Engine is a comprehensive gameplay scripting system built on the notion of creating gameplay pieces from within Unreal Editor utilizing a node-based interface. It defines object-oriented classes or objects in the engine, just like many other common scripting languages. When using UE4, you'll notice that objects defined with Blueprint are frequently referred to simply as "Blueprints."

This approach is very versatile and powerful because it allows designers to practically utilize the whole spectrum of concepts and techniques previously exclusively available to programmers. Furthermore, Blueprint-specific markup accessible in Unreal Engine's C++ implementation enables programmers to construct baseline systems that designers may enhance.

Does this imply that Blueprints have taken the role of UnrealScript? Both yes and no. Gameplay is programming, and everything else that UnrealScript was utilized for in the past can still be done using code in C++. At the same time, while Blueprints are not intended to be a substitute for UnrealScript, they do fulfill many of the same functions as UnrealScript, including:

- Classes are being expanded.

- Default properties are stored and modified.

- Managing the instancing of subobjects (for example, components) for classes.

It is expected that gameplay programmers would create basic classes that provide a valuable collection of methods and attributes that Blueprints derived from those base classes may utilize and extend upon.

To assist people moving from earlier versions of the engine, the table below compares how different elements would be handled in UnrealScript (from Unreal Engine 3), C++, and Blueprints. It also shows how native code and Blueprints compare.

UnrealScript (UE3)	Blueprints (UE4)	C++ (UE4)
.uc file	Blueprint Asset	.h/.cpp files
UClass	UBlueprintGeneratedClass	UClass
extends [ClassName]	ParentClass	: [ClassName]
Variable	Variable	UProperty()
Function	Graphs/Events	UFunction()
defaultproperties{}	Class Defaults	native constructor
Default Components	Components List	native constructor

BLUEPRINT VARIETIES

Blueprints can be of numerous types, each with its specific use, such as creating new types, scripting level events, or defining interfaces or macros for use by other Blueprints.

- **Blueprint Class:** A Blueprint Class, also known as a Blueprint, is an asset that allows content creators to add functionality on top of existing gameplay classes easily. Blueprints are generated graphically in Unreal Editor rather than by entering code and stored as assets in a content package. These effectively establish a new class or kind of Actor, which can subsequently be put as instances in maps and behave like any other form of Actor.

- **Data-Only Blueprint:** A data-only Blueprint is a Blueprint Class that simply includes the code (in node graphs), variables, and components passed down from its parent. These allow for the tweaking and modification of inherited attributes, but no new features may be introduced. These are essentially archetype replacements that will enable designers to alter attributes or configure objects with variants.

  Data-Only Blueprints may be updated in a compact property editor. Still, they can also be "converted" to complete Blueprints by simply adding code, variables, or components in the full Blueprint Editor.

- **Level Blueprint:** A Level Blueprint is a specific sort of Blueprint that serves as a global event graph for the whole level. Each level in your project comes with its Level Blueprint, which may be updated in the Unreal

Editor, but new Level Blueprints cannot be produced via the editor interface.

Function Calls or Flow Control operations are used to fire off sequences of actions related to the level as a whole or individual instances of Actors inside the level. This notion should be quite recognizable to anyone familiar with Unreal Engine 3, as it is very similar to how Kismet functioned in Unreal Engine 3.

Level Blueprints also serve as a command and control mechanism for level streaming and the Sequencer and for tying events to Actors placed within the level.

- **Blueprint Interface:** A Blueprint Interface is a collection of functions that may be attached to other Blueprints (name only, no implementation). Any Blueprint that includes the Interface is guaranteed to have those functionalities. The functionalities of the Interface can be assigned functionality in any Blueprint that provides for it. This is analogous to the idea of an interface in general programming, which allows many types of Objects to share and be accessible through a standard interface. Blueprint Interfaces, in a sense, enable various Blueprints to communicate and transfer data to one another.

  Blueprint Interfaces, like other Blueprints, may be created by content producers using the editor; however, they have certain limitations in that they cannot:

  - Create new variables.

  - Graphs should be edited.

  - Components should be added.

- **Blueprint Macro Library:** A Blueprint Macro Library is a collection of Macros or self-contained graphs used as nodes in other Blueprints. These can save time by storing frequently used node sequences complete with inputs and outputs for both execution and data transmission.

  Macros are shared by all graphs that reference them; however, they are auto-expanded into graphs during compilation as if they were a collapsed node. Blueprint Macro Libraries, as a result, do not need to be compiled. On the other hand, changes to a Macro are only reflected in graphs that reference that Macro when the Blueprint that contains those graphs is recompiled.

- **Blueprint Utilities:** A Blueprint Utility is an editor-only Blueprint that may be used to execute editor operations or expand editor capabilities. These can expose Events with no parameters as user interface (UI) buttons and run any functions exposed to Blueprints and operate on the current set of chosen Actors in the viewport.

ANATOMY OF THE BLUEPRINT

Blueprints' functionality is defined by different elements, some of which are present by default and others that may be added as needed. These let you construct Components, execute initialization and set up activities, respond to events, arrange and modularize operations, define properties, and do other things.

- **Window of Components:** With a basic grasp of Components, you can add Components to our Blueprint using the Components pane in the Blueprint

Editor. This allows for the addition of collision geometry via CapsuleComponents, BoxComponents, or SphereComponents, the addition of rendered geometry in the form of StaticMeshComponents or SkeletalMeshComponents, the control of movement via MovementComponents, and so on. The Components added to the Components list can also be given to instance variables, allowing them to be accessed in the graphs of this or other Blueprints.

- **Script for Construction:** When a Blueprint Class instance is generated, the Construction Script is executed after the Components list. It includes a node graph that is performed and allows the Blueprint Class instance to conduct initialization activities. This has the potential to be quite powerful since actions such as tracing into the environment, creating meshes and materials, and so on may be used to provide context-specific setup. For example, a light Blueprint might identify the type of ground it is put on and select the appropriate mesh from a collection of meshes or a fence. Blueprint might run traces in either direction to estimate how long a fence is required to cover the gap.

- **Graph of Events:** A Blueprint's EventGraph comprises a node graph that utilizes events and function calls to conduct actions in response to gameplay events related to the Blueprint. This is used to provide functionality that is shared by all Blueprint instances. This is where you put up interaction and dynamic reactions. A light Blueprint, for illustrate, might respond to a damage event by turning off its LightComponent and altering the material of its geometry. This would apply this behavior to all instances of the light Blueprint.

- **Functions:** Functions are node graphs that belong to a specific Blueprint and maybe run or called from another graph within the Blueprint. Functions have a single entry point identified by a node with the Method's name and have a single exec output pin. When calling the Function from the other graph, the output exec pin is enabled, forcing the linked network to execute.

- **Variables:** Variables are properties in the world that hold a value or relate to an Object or Actor. These attributes can be made accessible internally to the Blueprint that contains them, or they can be made accessible externally so that designers working with instances of the Blueprint put in a level can modify their values.

- **Modes of Blueprint:** The mode of a Blueprint controls what is seen in its window. Although Level Blueprints only have one way, the Graph mode, Blueprint Classes have three modes:

  - **Default Mode:** This is where you configure the Blueprint's settings.

  - **Components Mode:** This is where you add, delete, and change the components that comprise your Blueprint.

LOOKING FOR BLUEPRINTS

When we're in the Blueprint Editor, we can bring up the Find Results box by clicking on Search in the Toolbar or using Ctrl+F. You may use this page to search our Blueprints for nodes, pins, pin values, graphs, variables, and variable values that meet your search criteria. We may also search for animation graphs.

Right-clicking on a node in a Blueprint or an element in the My Blueprint window and selecting Find References will launch the Find Results window. The search box is pre-populated with the element's name and MemberGuid.

This guarantees that you are looking for that same variable or function, even if it appears numerous times in other areas of your code.

Searching is an asynchronous operation, which means that it may continue to use the editor while the search is running. We may also conduct numerous searches in several Blueprints at the same time. It uses the Asset Registry for searchable data; thus, the most recently indexed data is always included with the asset file.

By default, this tool searches our current Blueprint, but we may search all Blueprints in the project by unchecking the Find in Current Blueprint Only option. It will notify us if Blueprints are not indexed in the system.

The editor will stall when you click Index All as it loads all un-indexed Blueprints and re-saves them to cache searchable data. If we do not want to re-save the material, or if the content is controlled by source control and cannot be checked out, it will simply load all Blueprint assets in memory to cache the most recent searchable data. If we do not re-save the material, Index All must be performed each time we open the editor.

The Syntax for Advanced Search

Filters are an advanced search tool in Blueprints that allows you to target searches to particular subsets of data. We may, for example, isolate just Blueprints with nodes called something special or attributes with specific names and flags set. These may be layered and used to create sophisticated searches for particular requirements. Certain filters can only be used in conjunction with other filters; however, all filters can be used as a starting point. The following is a non-exhaustive list of searchable tags and the types of data they are used for. Without the usage of filters, all tags may be searched for.

Some objects can only be searched for using tags, which helps to avoid clutter while searching without tags. These objects are labeled with (Explicit). Filtering is currently limited to user-added member variables.

Nodes(Name=Coin) is a sample search string that will discover all nodes in the Blueprint with the word "coin" in the name.

Filter	Searchable Tags	Subfilters
Blueprint	• Name	• Graphs
	• ParentClass	• Functions
	• Path	• Macros
	• Interfaces	• EventGraphs
		• Nodes
		• Pins
		• Variables
		• Components

(Continued)

Filter	Searchable Tags	Subfilters
• Graphs	• Name	• Nodes
• Functions	• Description	• Pins
• Macros		• Variables
• EventGraphs		
Nodes	• Name	Pins
	• ClassName	
	• Comment	
• Pins	• Name	
• Variables/	• DefaultValue	
Properties	• IsArray	
• Components	• IsReference	
	• IsSCSComponent	
	• PinCategory	
	• ObjectClass	

All Subfilter

Everything is a special subfilter. When nested in another filter, it allows any data included to be checked against all children of any objects that would typically pass the filter.

Graphs(Name=MyFunction && All(Return)) is an example.

Any graph with the name "MyFunction" will search for the string "Return" in all of its descendants (nodes, local variables, and pins).

Classes on the Blueprint

A Blueprint Class, often known as a Blueprint, is a type of asset that allows content producers to build functionality on top of existing gameplay classes quickly. Blueprints are generated graphically in Unreal Editor rather than by entering code and stored as assets in a content package.

These effectively establish a new class or kind of Actor, which can subsequently be put as instances in maps and behave like any other form of Actor.

Blueprint Components

Blueprints don't necessarily have to have programmed behavior. A light post in our level, for example, may not be interactive and may only require a mesh to depict the post and a lamp. Using Components to create reusable Blueprints would speed up the level creation process. Of course, we could use those Components in a graph to enable our players to interact with the lights, or we could have a time-of-day system modify them appropriately.

Blueprint Graphs

Graphs depict your Blueprints' design-time and game-time behavior. When an instance of a Blueprint Class is produced, the Construction Script runs after the Components list, allowing you to dynamically modify the appearance and feel of the new Object or Actor.

A Blueprint's EventGraph comprises a node graph that utilizes events and function calls to conduct actions in response to gameplay events related to the Blueprint. This is used to provide functionality that is shared by all Blueprint instances. This is where we put up interaction and dynamic reactions. A light Blueprint, for example, might respond to a damage event by turning off its LightComponent and altering the material of its geometry. This would apply this behavior to all instances of the light Blueprint.

Blueprint Creation

There are various ways to build Blueprints. The first is to use the Content Browser and click the Add New button:

- Click the Add New button in the Content Browser.

- Blueprint Class should be selected from the Create Basic Asset portion of the dropdown menu.

- For our Blueprint Asset, select a Parent Class. After choosing our class, a new Blueprint asset will be added to the Content Browser, which we may then name.

Using Assets, Create a Blueprint

- We can also build a Blueprint by right-clicking an asset in the Content Browser and selecting the Create Blueprint Using This... option from the Asset Actions menu.

- We will be requested to save the Blueprint after selecting the Create Blueprint Using This... option. After we confirm our save location, the Blueprint will open in the Blueprint Editor.

Putting Blueprints in Different Levels

- We have two options for placing a Blueprint in our level.

- Drag and drop it into our level using the Content Browser.

- Alternatively, with the Blueprint selected in the Content Browser, right-click on the level and choose Place Actor from the context menu.

Putting Blueprint Nodes in Place

- There are numerous ways to put nodes in Graph Mode; this section will show us the most popular approach and connect nodes.

- The Context Menu, which Right-clicking inside a Blueprint graph can access, will be used most of the time when inserting nodes.

- We may expand any category (or subcategory) and pick the node we add to the graph from the menu above.

- There is also a Context-Sensitive option in the top right corner of the window that is enabled by default but can be deactivated and automatically filters the options shown in the menu based on the current context.

- When we right-click and search for Animation with Context-Sensitive turned on, we'll see a filtered list.

- If we uncheck Context-Sensitive and search for Animation, we will see anything connected to animation.

- While right-clicking in the graph brings up the Context Menu, we can also reach the Context Menu by dragging off an existing node.

- We have a Character Movement Component Reference, and by pulling off its out pin, we can add nodes that are contextually related to the node we are dragging off of.

- We may change the Max Walk Speed of the character by searching for Set Max Walk and then selecting Set Max Walk Speed from the menu.

Blueprint Node Connections

To link nodes, drag one pin off and attach it to another pin of the same type (there are some instances where a conversion node will be created, for example, connecting a Float output to a Text input will create a conversion node between the two and automatically convert and connect the two nodes).

Making Variables

Variables are properties in the world that hold a value or relate to an Object or Actor. These attributes can be made accessible internally to the Blueprint that contains them, or they can be made accessible externally so that designers working with instances of the Blueprint put in a level can modify their values.

From the MyBlueprint window, we can add variables to your Blueprints by selecting the Add Button (+) on the variable list heading.

Once we've established a variable, we'll need to be able to define its attributes.

Combining Blueprints with C++

There is no conundrum. If at all feasible, your project should make advantage of both. Blueprint visual scripting was not intended to replace C++ while being an excellent type of scripting altogether. It enables individuals who are not programmers to write the game's logic.

Yes, a game may be finished and published using only blueprints.

If we're a hobbyist, single developer, or simply learning to make games, a blueprint-only project might be an excellent way to get started. There's a lot to learn in game development, so bypassing standard programming languages at the start would be a significant time-saver. Furthermore, not everyone's intellect is capable of effortlessly digesting text-based programming. Visual scripting is more suited to the minds of artists, level designers, and writers.

A programmer, on the other hand, is usually part of a team. Or a large number of them.

We may easily combine the two options if we have programmers on your staff or anybody who spends some time on C++ programming. Visual scripting is intended to augment text-based programming/scripting by freeing programmers from scripting tasks that content creators may readily perform.

Why Do Projects Still Require Traditional Programming and Programmers?

- Scripting languages are usually less efficient than C++ code: they execute slower and consume more memory.

  - However, the performance impact of the blueprint script would be minimal most of the time. There are several frequent performance traps in blueprints that we cannot avoid by following Fundamental Blueprint Practices.

  - Jumbled blueprints cause more considerable difficulties, frequently generated by persons who only deal with visual programming. Simply put, they were never allowed to learn programming ideas and techniques. These might have a significant influence on iteration timelines and the overall quality of the codebase. Yes, building code from nodes can be rapid, but sloppy code causes technical debt since it's challenging to work with or develop new features.

- Individuals who utilize blueprints can certainly learn proper programming, but because blueprints are so simple to use, many people choose to write things "however it just works." "Anyway" is frequently a poor manner. Destructive code simply implies that it is difficult to comprehend, even for the creator. Changing minor details in a messy code takes significantly longer and is more error-prone. If the code is overly complex and poorly designed, it is pretty easy to introduce errors.

- Learning any standard programming language aids in learning how to utilize blueprints efficiently. Even studying C# in Unity would be beneficial because it will introduce you to programming principles.

- Node-based scripting provides just a fraction of the options available in the underlying programming language. Blueprints provide so much Unreal C++ functionality that it is feasible to create prototypes and a significant portion of the game programming using nodes. Nonetheless, it is just a subset of the general-purpose, multi-paradigm language known as C++.

- Only items that have been exposed to the Unreal Property System (Reflection) can be exposed to blueprints. We can only utilize in blueprints the data types and C++ capabilities that Epic manages in the engine. We may believe that we have no deficiencies in designs just because we are unaware of C++ capabilities.

- In practice, not every built-in feature of C++ can be available to blueprints, for example, Programming Subsystems.

- Blueprints support only Object-Oriented Programming. Every blueprint represents some type of "object" descended from the UObject class. Checks see Basic Object Classes see where "actor" and "components" fit in. This arrangement is relatively natural and straightforward for constructing virtual worlds (after all, everything in the actual world is a type of object, right?). Still, it is not the only method to program.

- Slate, the UI framework used to construct the editor UI, employs a different programming paradigm known as "declarative syntax." Slate cannot exist in blueprints since there are no UObjects. Only C++ and Slate allow for the creation and customization of editor UI.

- UMG develops an in-game UI, which is Slate accessible to UObjects through a specific class named UWidget. Every in-game element generated using UMG is a "widget," a type of object that cannot be put in the actual world.

- People who don't know even the most fundamental C++ are unable to read and debug engine code.

It implies they'll never grasp what happens in the engine or when the provided function in blueprints is invoked. They can only imagine how the game works; therefore, they require assistance from a coder. Engine documentation and the Internet will never be able to address all of your questions.

- As a result, the team will not alter the engine code, which is a standard procedure when working with Unreal. It's completely optional, but it's convenient.

    - A slight modification in the engine code may enable implementing a game-specific feature that would otherwise be impossible. The team would have to abandon that functionality or develop it sloppily (workaround for unmodified engine code).

    - Bugs and crashes in the engine may be easily fixed. Changing a few lines of code is frequently all that is required. That might be crucial when the game is ready to be launched—we just need to release the game on the current engine version, but there are some major engine issues to address.

    - Sometimes "changes from the future," a relatively minor engine from the engine's developer branch, can be simply integrated (a bugfix or improvement to some system).

- The preceding statement also applies to the code of plugins obtained through the marketplace. Many plugins' code isn't flawless, and it occasionally necessitates debugging and changes.

THE BENEFITS OF BLUEPRINTS

- **Prototyping in a Hurry:** With in-editor tools like blueprints, it's incredibly simple to prototype mechanics, events, and any other wacky concept. This is something that non-programmers can accomplish. Instead of wasting time writing documentation with new ideas and attempting to convey them to programmers, simply execute our ideas. It's often enough to start putting together plans to realize that a particular notion won't work. While implementing it, we must discard it or redesign it. We don't have to wait for a programmer, and we don't spend programmer time creating vague notions that are frequently hard to describe at this point entirely.

- **Working with Assets:** A blueprint is a code combination (each blueprint is a class based on UObject) and data. It's natural and straightforward to connect any assets in blueprint code, such as materials, textures, audio, and so on. In text-based programming, the same thing may be highly time-consuming. Often, programmers would have to construct a new variable merely to acquire an asset reference, hardcode the path to the asset (which means the code would have to be manually updated if the asset name changed...), or build support that served as a list of other assets.

- **A Small Amount of Scripting:** Any single actor programming, such as how the door behaves or occurs when the player interacts with the chest. In extensively directed games, there are dozens, even hundreds of such scripts. Every unique object, every minute of the game, and every location on the map has its script that enhances the experience. Hide such things in C++ would be useless and counter-productive. However, it is suggested to specify a base of standard classes (for example, NPC, spawner, door, a box with treasure) in code—providing simple interoperability across systems developed in C++.

- **UI and Animation Scripting:** Animation blueprints allow developers to script animation states. And use UMG blueprints to create UI. Control Rig, the procedural animation technology, is also primarily based on blueprints.

- **Simple Scripting in the Editor:** Some editor activities can be scripted using editor blueprints. Although Python, a language frequently used in art/VFX applications, may now be utilized for editor programming.

C++'S BENEFITS

- **Algorithms and Complex Math:** Assembling sophisticated logic in visual scripting is time-consuming and inconvenient. This would require a lot of clicking in blueprints, nodes would not fit in the window (it is difficult to operate on large node networks), and runtime speed would suffer. While doing the same thing in C++ with only a few lines of text would be far faster.

- **All Engine and Programming Features Are Available:** We don't develop game code in raw C++; instead, we utilize "Unreal C++." Epic has enhanced C++ with its own core C++ library, which is suited for video game development. Please see a separate page for more information on Unreal C++.

- **The Majority of the Engine Is Written in Unreal C++:** We will already understand the engine code if we know how to create C++ for your game.

- **Capability to Code UI Modifications and Custom Editors:** In UE4, hundreds of editors specialize in a particular game system. Our is what makes this engine such a rich collection of creative tools. Nothing prevents us from developing our project-specific editors, which might be a massive benefit to our team.

- **Blueprints Are Classified as Binary Assets:** It is not possible to combine blueprints. It is possible to view a blueprints version diff, but only in visual form (two graphs displayed side by side). Complex blueprint refactoring takes additional time. Blueprints aren't a good option for essential code sections that are at the heart of your gameplay.

- **Systems:** C++ is the sole language in which gaming systems should be implemented for all of the reasons stated above. It provides quick iteration rates, superior performance, and complete control over what is available to non-programmer users.

- **Efficient Implementation of Networked Games:** Blueprints may manage a wide range of multiplayer capabilities, including replication, code-only server or client execution, and much more. The Gameplay Ability System enables designers to take advantage of sophisticated multiplayer API that is not easily accessible via blueprints. However, multiplayer games offer an entirely new dimension to game production. Every object, function, and piece of data must be taken into account.

BLUEPRINT AND C++ COMPATIBILITY

One of the primary considerations when designing the overall technical design for a game is what should be done in Blueprints and what should be implemented in C++. The goal of this is to investigate how to answer these types of questions and to make advice on how to build data-driven solid gaming systems. This topic is intended for programmers or technical designers who have already studied essential programming documentation and want to learn more. There is no single "correct" method to create a game, but this guide will help us ask the appropriate questions.

Data and Logic in Gameplay

Things in a game may be split into two categories: logic and data. The rules and structure followed by sections of your game are referred to as gameplay logic, whereas gameplay data is used by the logic and explains what the game does. This divide is sometimes visible, like when the C++ code used to render a character on screen is logic-based while the physical look is data-based. However, these groups might blend, adding complexity to our project, so it's critical to grasp the distinction and our alternatives.

There are a few ways for adding gameplay logic into Unreal Engine 4 (UE4):

- **C++ Classes:** Variables and functions are created in C++ and are responsible for implementing the basic gameplay logic.

- **Blueprint Classes:** Logic may be implemented in the Blueprint Event Graph or by calling functions from those graphs. Additional variables can also be added.

- **Customized Systems:** Many systems and games include minor "micro languages" that express some part of gaming logic. Custom systems for storing gameplay logic include the UE4 Materials Editor, Sequencer Tracks, and AI Behavior Trees.

You have additional possibilities for Data:

- **C++ Classes:** Native class constructors establish default values and allow data inheritance in C++. Data can be hard-coded into local function variables as well, although this is difficult to track.

- **Config Files:** Ini files and Console Variables allow you to override data specified in C++ constructors or query them directly.

- **Blueprint Classes:** Blueprint class defaults are similar to C++ class constructors in that they enable data inheritance. Data can also be stored safely in function local variables or as literal pin values.

- **Data Assets:** Standalone Data Assets are more accessible to utilize than Blueprint Defaults for things that cannot be instanced and do not require data inheritance.

- **Tables:** Imported data might be in the form of Data Tables, Curve Tables, or runtime reads.

- **Placed Instances:** Data may be saved in instances of Blueprint or C++ classes placed inside levels or other assets, and these instances will override the class defaults.

- **Custom Systems:** Just like logic, there are several custom methods for storing data. Runtime saves game files can be used to override or change the data types listed above.

The derived choices farther down these lists usually override and expand the base-level options above them. As a result, it is difficult for base-level systems to access and use items described by extended systems. Accessing a variable introduced by a Blueprint Class from a C++ Class, for example, is highly complex and should be avoided. To avoid issues like these, define functions and variables at the most fundamental level where they will often be used. It may make sense to implement Logic fully at the base level, or you may leave a stub function at the base level and override it at a higher level.

Because there are more choices and more profound inheritance is more prevalent, the rules for Data are more sophisticated and system-specific. We must specify default values for variables at the level at which they were declared, and any higher-level derived levels can overrule them. It is also typical to build logic that copies data based on specific rules from one object to another.

BLUEPRINTS VS. C++

We'll see in the above lists that either C++ or Blueprint classes may be utilized to hold Logic and Data. Most gaming features will be implemented in one way due to this versatility (or in some combination). There is no "correct decision" when selecting whether to use C++ or Blueprint because each game and development team is unique, but here are some basic principles to assist you in deciding whether to use C++ or Blueprint:

Benefits of the C++ Class

- **Faster Runtime Performance:** C++ logic is often much quicker than Blueprint logic, for reasons that will be discussed more below.

- **Explicit Design:** When exposing variables or functions from C++, we have more control over exactly what we want to expose, allowing you to protect particular methods/variables and build a formal "API" for our class. This enables us to avoid building Blueprints that are too big and difficult to follow.

- **Broader Access:** Functions and variables written in C++ (and appropriately exposed) may be accessed from any other system, making it ideal for transferring data between systems. Furthermore, C++ exposes more engine functionality than Blueprints.

- **More Data Control:** When it comes to loading and storing data, C++ has access to more unique features. This enables us to manage version updates and serialization in a highly customized manner.

- **Network Replication:** Blueprints' replication capability is simple and intended to be utilized in smaller games or for one-of-a-kind Actors. If we require precise control over replication bandwidth or time, C++ is the way to go.

- **Better for Arithmetic:** Consider using C++ for math-heavy tasks because doing sophisticated math in Blueprints may be difficult and time-consuming; consider using C++ for math-heavy tasks.

- **More Accessible to Diff/Merge:** C++ code and data (as well as configuration and perhaps bespoke solutions) are kept as text, making it easier to work in several branches simultaneously.

ADVANTAGES OF THE BLUEPRINT CLASS

- **Faster Creation:** For most individuals, building a new Blueprint class and adding variables and methods is more rapid than doing the same thing in C++; therefore, developing brand new systems with Blueprint is frequently faster.

- **Faster Iteration:** Changing Blueprint logic and previewing it inside the editor is considerably quicker than recompiling the game, but hot reloading can assist. This is true for both mature and young systems; consequently, if possible, all "tweakable" values should be maintained in assets.

- **Better For Flow:** Because it might be difficult to perceive "game flow" in C++, it is frequently preferable to create it in Blueprints (or in custom systems like Behavior Trees designed for this). Using delay and async nodes makes following flow easier than using C++ delegates.

- **Flexible Editing:** Blueprints may be created and edited by designers and artists without technical knowledge, making them perfect for assets that need to be updated by more than just engineers.

- **Easier Data Usage:** Storing data within Blueprint classes is considerably simpler and safer than keeping data inside C++ classes; Blueprints are ideal for classes that blend data and logic.

BLUEPRINT TO C++ CONVERSION

Because Blueprints are easy to develop and iterate on, it is usual to design prototypes in Blueprint before moving some or all of the functionality into C++. We should typically do this after we've proven the essential operation and wish to "solidify" it, so that other people may use it without breaking it. We'll need to determine which classes, functions, and variables should be moved to C++ and which should remain in Blueprint at this stage. Before making that decision, it's a good idea to understand the process of refactoring things into C++.

The first step is to construct a collection of "Base" C++ classes from which our Blueprint classes will inherit. After generating our game's foundation native classes, we'll need to reparent any prototype Blueprints to your new native classes. After that, we can begin transferring variables and functions from our Blueprint classes into native C++. If a variable or method in our native class has the same type and name as a variable in the Blueprint, we should update the Blueprint's external references to point to the native base classes.

CONCERNS ABOUT PERFORMANCE

Performance is one of the primary reasons to prefer C++ over Blueprints. In many situations, though, Blueprint performance is not an issue in reality. The primary distinction is that running each node in a Blueprint is slower than executing a line of C++ code, but once within a node, execution is just as quick as if it were called from C++. For example, if our Blueprint class includes a few low-cost top-level nodes and then uses a costly Physics Trace method, switching it to C++ will not significantly increase speed.

However, if our Blueprint class has a lot of tight for loops or nested macros that extend into hundreds of nodes, we should consider transferring that code to C++. Tick functions will be one of the most significant performance issues. Blueprint tick execution can be significantly slower than native tick execution, and we should avoid tick altogether for any class with numerous instances. Instead, we should use timers or delegates to ensure that our Blueprint class only does tasks when required.

The Profiler Tool is the best approach to determine whether your Blueprint classes are creating performance issues. To understand where performance is going in your project, first create a circumstance in which our Blueprint classes are significantly straining performance (for example, generating a slew of opponents), then record a profile using the Profiler tool. We may use the Profiler tool to explore the Game Thread Tick and grow the tree until we discover specific Blueprint classes (it may group all instances of the same class together, so keep that in mind).

Within the Blueprint classes, you can extend the Blueprint function that is taking too long. If we spend most of our time in Self, we are losing performance because of Blueprint overhead. However, if most of the time is spent in other native events nested within the function, then your Blueprint overhead is not an issue.

Blueprint Nativization can help to alleviate many of these issues, but it is not without disadvantages. For starters, it alters our cook workflow, which can impede iteration on cooked games. Furthermore, because the runtime logic for nativized Blueprints differs from that of conventional Blueprints, we may see various problems or behavior based on the details of our game.

Most Blueprint features are entirely supported in nativization, although certain esoteric ones may not be. Finally, the speed increase will not be as substantial as if we had changed it to C++. Nativization may not address all of our performance concerns, but it should be examined as a possible solution.

NOTES ON ARCHITECTURE

When creating a game that mixes Blueprints and C++, we will face difficulties as our game grows in size and complexity. Here are some things to bear in mind when a project begins to take shape:

- **Avoid Casting to Expensive Blueprints:** Casting to a Blueprint class BP A (or declaring it as a variable type on a function or other Blueprint) establishes a load dependence on that Blueprint. If BP A refers to four big Static Meshes and 20 noises, BP B will have to load four large Static Meshes and 20 sounds every time loaded, even if the cast fails. This is one of the main reasons it's critical to have native base classes or basic Blueprint base classes that specify the relevant functions and variables. Then, create our costly Blueprints as child classes.

- **Avoid Cyclical Blueprint References:** Because of header files, cyclical references (where a class references another class, which references the original class) are not a problem with C++. Excessive cyclical Blueprint references, on the other hand, might increase editor load and build time. Similar to the previous point, this may be improved by casting to C++ classes or cheaper Base Blueprint classes instead of casting to expensive child Blueprints (or having variable references).

- **Minimize Using Assets from C++ Classes:** It is feasible to use FObjectFinder and FClassFinder to reference assets from C++ constructors, but this should be avoided whenever possible. Assets referenced in this manner are loaded at project launch, causing load time and memory concerns if the references are not required. Furthermore, assets referred to by constructors cannot be readily removed or renamed. In general, instead of referring to particular Static Meshes from C++, it's a good idea to construct some "Game Data" assets or Blueprint types and load them via the asset management or config file.

- **Avoid Referencing Assets by String:** To avoid problems with loading assets from C++ classes, we can use C++ methods like LoadObject to load a specific object on a disc explicitly. However, because these references are entirely untracked by the chef, they may cause issues in packed games. Instead, in our C++ classes, you should utilize FSoftObjectPath or

TSoftObjectPtr types, configure them from ini or Blueprint classes, and then load them on-demand or via async loading.

- **Be Cautious While Using User Structs and Enums:** C++-defined enums and structs can be used by both C++ and Blueprints, but user structs/enums cannot be used in C++ and cannot be manually patched up as stated in the save game section. We advocate implementing essential enums and structs in C++ since we may wish to shift more of your gameplay logic to C++ in the future. If anything is used by more than one or two Blueprints, it should be implemented in native C++.

- **Consider Network Architecture:** The network architecture of your game will have a significant impact on how you build our classes. Prototypes are not often created with networking in mind, so when we begin reworking things to be "real," we must consider which Actors will be duplicating which data. To design a successful flow for replicated data, we may need to make decisions that make it more difficult to iterate on.

- **Consider Async Loading:** As our game develops in size, we'll want to load assets on demand rather than loading everything at once when the game loads. We should start changing items to utilize Soft references or PrimaryAssetIds instead of Hard references when we get to this stage. The AssetManager exposes a StreamableManager that provides lower-level operations and many functions to enable async loading assets.

BLUEPRINTS PROGRAMMING GUIDELINES

When selecting whether to utilize C++ or Blueprints, two factors must be considered:

1. Speed

2. Expression complexity

Aside from those two criteria, a lot of it comes down to the difficulty of the game and the squad makeup. If we have many more artists than programmers, you will undoubtedly have far more Blueprints than C++ code. In contrast, if we have many programmers, they are likely to prefer to retain things in C++. We anticipate that most people will fall somewhere in the center. Much of the workflow at Epic is that content producers will create a complicated Blueprint, and a programmer will realize how they can condense a lot of that work into C++ by writing a new Blueprint node, so they transfer that chunk of functionality into a new C++ function. A smart approach would be to utilize Blueprints widely and then push things into C++ as they reach a level of complexity that allows for a more succinct description of the functionality (or it gets too complicated for a non-programmer) or when the speed of execution demands a shift to C++.

- **Speed:** In terms of performance, Blueprint execution is slower than C++ execution. That's not to imply performance is terrible, but if we're doing anything that requires a lot of calculations or operates at a high frequency, C++ may be preferable to Blueprints. However, it is feasible to mix the two to benefit your team and the overall success of your project. If we have a Blueprint with a lot of functionality, we can move a portion of it to C++ to speed it up while keeping the rest in Blueprints to preserve flexibility.

If our profiling reveals that one action in Blueprints takes a long time, try converting only that piece into C++ and leaving the remainder in Blueprints.

A crowd system that controls a thousand Actors is an example of a system that would take a long time to run using Blueprint visual programming. In this scenario, it would be preferable to handle crowd decision making, pathing, and other crowd functionality in C++ and then expose specific modifying parameters and controlling methods to Blueprints.

- **Expression Complexity:** A few things in C++ are more straightforward to accomplish than in Blueprints in terms of expression complexity. Blueprints are great for many things, but certain things are just tricky to represent in nodes. Operating on big data sets, string manipulation, complicated math over vast data sets, and so on are all highly complex and challenging to follow in a visual system. Those are best preserved in C++ rather than Blueprints since they are easier to look at and figure out what's going on. Another reason a crowd system might be better implemented in C++ code rather than Blueprints is the complexity of expression in Unreal Engine.

CHAPTER 4

Blackboard and Behavior Tree with AI

ARTIFICIAL INTELLIGENCE (AI)

AI in video games often refers to how a non-player character makes decisions. This may be as easy as an opponent seeing the gamer and then assaulting. It might also be something more complicated, such as an AI-controlled player in a real-time strategy. You may construct AI in Unreal Engine by utilizing behavior trees. A behavior tree is a mechanism for determining which actions an AI should do. You might, for example, have a fight-and-run behavior. You might program the AI's behavior tree such that it fights if its health exceeds 50%. If it is less than 50%, it will flee.

DOI: 10.1201/9781003214731-4

In this section, we will learn how to:

- Create an AI creature capable of controlling a Pawn.

- Make and employ behavior trees and blackboards.

- To give the Pawn sight, use AI Perception.

- Create behaviors that allow the Pawn to move about and attack opponents.

Getting Going

Unzip the starting project https://koenig-media.ray-wenderlich.com/uploads/2017/12/MuffinWarStarter.zip after downloading it. Navigate to the project folder and double-click MuffinWar.uproject to launch it. To begin the game, press the play button and spawn a muffin left-click within the enclosed area.

We will program an AI to walkabout. When an enemy muffin enters the AI's field of view, the AI will move to it and assault it.

Three elements are required to build an AI character:

1. **Body:** This is the character's physical depiction. The muffin serves as the body in this example.

2. **Soul:** The soul is the entity that controls the character. This might be the player or a computerized AI.

3. **Brain:** The brain is where the AI makes choices. This may be done in various methods, including C++ code, Blueprints, and behavior trees.

We already have a body; therefore, all you need is a soul and a brain. To begin, we will construct a controller, which will serve as the soul.

What Exactly Is a Controller?

A controller is a non-physical actor who has control over a Pawn. Possession allows the controller to control the Pawn, as you might expect. But what exactly does the term "control" entail in this context?

For the player, this entails pushing a button and instructing the Pawn to do something. The controller accepts input from the player and then sends it to the Pawn. Instead, the controller might process the inputs and then instruct the Pawn to perform actions.

In the case of AI, the Pawn can receive information from the controller or brain (depending on how you program it).

To use AI to control the muffins, we must first develop a specific controller known as an AI controller (AIC).

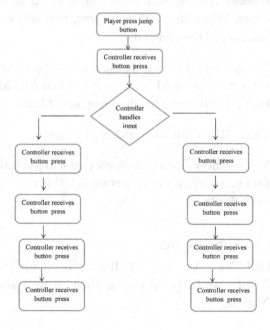

Developing an AIC

- Create a new Blueprint Class by going to Characters\ Muffin\AI. Choose AIC as the parent class and give it the name AIC_Muffin.

- You must next instruct the muffin to utilize your new AIC. Open BP_Muffin from the CharactersMuffinBlueprints folder.

- The Details section should display the Blueprint's default settings by default. If it doesn't, go to the Toolbar and choose Class Defaults.

- Navigate to the Details panel and look for the Pawn section. AIC Muffin should be selected as the AIC Class. When the muffin spawns, this will create an instance of the controller.

- Because you're spawning the muffins, you should also set Auto Possess AI to Spawned. When AIC Muffin is born, it will immediately possess BP Muffin.

- Close BP Muffin after clicking Compile.

- You will now develop the logic that will guide the muffin's behavior. We may accomplish this by employing behavior trees.

Making a Behavior Tree

Select Add New\Artificial Intelligence\Behavior Tree from the Characters\Muffin\AI menu. Then, open it and name it BT Muffin.

The Editor of the Behavior Tree

Two new panels have been added to the behavior tree editor:

- **Behavior Tree:** In this graph, you will build nodes that will form the behavior tree.

  - **Details:** The attributes of the nodes you pick will be displayed here.

- **Blackboard:** This panel displays Blackboard keys and their values. It only appears when the game is running.

Behavior trees, like Blueprints, are made up of nodes. In behavior trees, there are four sorts of nodes. Tasks and composites are the first two.

What Exactly Are Tasks and Composites?

A task, as the name indicates, is a node that "does" something. This might be something complicated, like performing a combination. It might even be something as easy as sitting and waiting.

To do out tasks, you must employ composites. A behavior tree is made up of several branches (the behaviors). Each branch has a composite at its root. Different types of composites execute their child nodes in different ways.

For instance, take the following sequence of events:

A Sequence composite would be used to conduct each action in a sequence. This is due to the fact that a Sequence executes its offspring from left to right. Here's how it might look:

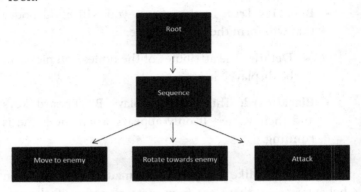

If any of a Sequence's offspring fail, the Sequence will be terminated.

Move To Enemy, for instance, will fail if the Pawn is unable to move to the enemy. This implies that Rotate Towards Enemy and Attack will both fail to perform. They will, nevertheless, execute if the Pawn is successful in advancing to the enemy.

We will also learn about the Selector composite later on. For the time being, we will use a Sequence to move the Pawn to a random place and then wait.

Moving to an Unpredictable Location

- Make a Sequence and link it to the Root.

- The next step is to move the Pawn. Make a MoveTo and link it to Sequence. This node will direct the Pawn to a certain actor or area.

- Create a Wait and attach it to Sequence after that. Make sure it's to the right of MoveTo. Because the children will operate from left to right, order is essential.

- We've just programmed our first behavior! It will move the Pawn to a certain place and then wait five seconds.

- We must provide a location to move the Pawn. However, MoveTo only accepts values from blackboards, so we must construct one.

Making a Blackboard

A chalkboard is a piece of equipment whose main purpose is to hold variables (known as keys). It may be thought of as the AI's memory.

While they are not essential, blackboards provide a simple way to read and store data. It's useful since many nodes in behavior trees only take blackboard keys.

Return to the Content Browser and choose Add New\ Artificial Intelligence\Blackboard. Then, open it and name it BB_Muffin.

The Editor of Blackboard

The blackboard editor is made up of two frames:

- **Keys:** This panel will show us a list of your keys.

- **Blackboard Details:** The attributes of the chosen key will be displayed in this panel.

We must now build a key that will contain the target location.

Making a Target Location Key

Because we are storing a position in 3D space, it must be stored as a vector. Select Vector from the New Key menu. Give it the name TargetLocation.

Then we'll need a method to generate a random position and save it to the blackboard. We may accomplish this by employing the third type of behavior tree node: service.

What Exactly Is a Service?

Services are similar to tasks in that we utilize them to complete a task. Instead of requiring the Pawn to do an action, we utilize services to conduct checks or update the blackboard.

Services are not isolated nodes. They instead connect to tasks or composites. Because there are fewer nodes to deal with, the behavior tree becomes more ordered.

Making a Service

- Return to BT Muffin and choose New Service.

- This will instantly establish new service and launch it. BTService SetRandomLocation is its name. We must return to the Content Browser to rename it.

- The service is only required to run when the Pawn wishes to move. Attach it to MoveTo to do this.

- Right-click on MoveTo after opening BT_Muffin. Select Add Service\BTService Set Random Location from the menu.

- BTService_SetRandomLocation will now be activated when MoveTo is activated.

- The next step is to choose a random target location.

Creating a Location at Random

- Enable BTService_SetRandomLocation.

- Create an Event Receive Activation AI node to be notified when the service is activated. When the service's parent (the node to which it is connected) activates, this will be executed.

- Add the marked nodes to produce a random location. Make sure the Radius is set to 500.

- This will provide a randomly generated navigable place within 500 units of the Pawn.

- After that, we must record the position on the chalkboard. There are two methods for indicating which key to use:

  - In a Make Literal Name node, you may define the key by specifying its name.

  - We may make a variable available to the behavior tree. We will be able to choose a key from a dropdown list as a result of this.

We will use the second approach. Make a variable of the Blackboard Key Selector type. Name it BlackboardKey and check the box for Instance Editable. When we choose the service in the behavior tree, the variable will show.

- **Create the Highlighted Nodes Next:** Activation of an Event when its parent (in this example, MoveTo) activates, AI executes.

The function GetRandomPointInNavigableRadius delivers a random navigable point within 500 units of the controlling muffin.

Set the Blackboard Value to Vector assigns a random place to the value of a blackboard key (given by BlackboardKey).

Close BTService SetRandomLocation after clicking Compile.

The next step is to instruct the behavior tree to utilize our blackboard.

Choosing a Blackboard

Make sure we don't have anything selected in BT_Muffin. Navigate to the Details panel. Set Blackboard Asset to BB_Muffin in the Behavior Tree.

Following that, MoveTo and BTService_SetRandomLocation will utilize the first blackboard key. It is TargetLocation in this case.

Finally, we must instruct the AIC to execute the behavior tree.

Executing the Behavior Tree

- Connect a Run Behavior Tree to Event BeginPlay in AIC_Muffin. BTAsset should be set to BT_Muffin.

- When AIC_Controller spawns, this will launch BT_Muffin.

- Return to the main editor by clicking Compile. Play the game, generate some muffins, and watch them run about.

That took a lot of planning, but we made it. The AIC will then be configured such that it can identify adversaries inside its field of vision. We may accomplish this by utilizing AI Perception.

Constructing AI Perception

AI Perception is a component that actors can have. You may use it to give your AI senses (such as sight and hearing).

AIC_Muffin should be opened, and then an AI Perception component should be added.

After that, we must include a sense. We'll need to add a sight sense if we wish to detect when another muffin comes into view.

Go to the Details section after selecting AI Perception. Add a new element to Senses Config under AI Perception.

Set AI Sight config to element 0 and then expand it.

Sight may be adjusted in three ways:

1. **Sight Radius:** The muffin's sight radius is the farthest distance he or she can see. Set this to 3000.

2. **Lose Sight Radius:** If the muffin sees an adversary, this is the distance the enemy must go before the muffin loses sight of it. Set this to 3500.

3. **Vision in the Periphery Half Angle Degrees:** The breadth of the muffin's vision. Set this to 45 degrees. This gives the muffin a 90-degree field of vision.

AI Perception recognizes only opponents by default (actors assigned to a different team). Actors, on the other hand, do not have a team by default. When an actor lacks a team, AI Perception considers them neutral.

As of this writing, there is no way to allocate teams using Blueprints. Instead, you may simply instruct AI Perception to recognize neutral actors. To do so, expand Detection by Affiliation and check the box next to Detect Neutrals.

Return to the main editor by clicking Compile. Press the Play button to start spawning muffins. To access the AI debug screen, use the 'key. To see AI Perception, press 4 on the numpad. A green sphere will form as a muffin moves into view.

The muffin will then be moved toward an adversary. To do this, the behavior tree must be aware of the enemy. We may do this by making a note of the opponent on the chalkboard.

Building an Enemy Key

Open BB_Muffin and then add an Object key. Change the name to Enemy.

We will not be able to utilize Enemy in a MoveTo right now. This is due to the fact that the key is an Object, but MoveTo only takes keys of the Vector or Actor types.

To remedy this, go to Enemy and then Key Type. Change the Base Class to Actor. Enemy will be recognized as an Actor by the behavior tree as a result of this.

BB_Muffin, please close. We must now devise a strategy for approaching an adversary.

Approaching an Enemy

Open BT_Muffin and then unplug Sequence and Root. We may do so by alt-clicking the cable that connects them. Set aside the roam subtree for the time being.

Create the indicated nodes and assign them the Blackboard Key Enemy:

This will cause the Pawn to advance toward the Enemy. In certain circumstances, the Pawn will not fully face its target, thus we must additionally utilize Rotate to face the BB entrance.

When AI Perception discovers another muffin, we must now set Enemy.

Activating the Enemy Key

Select the AI Perception component in AIC_Muffin. Add a new event called On Perception Updated.

This event will be triggered if a sensation is updated. When the AI sees or loses sight of anything in this situation. This event also delivers a list of actors that it is presently aware of.

Add the nodes that were highlighted. Make sure that Make Literal Name is set to Enemy.

This will determine whether the AI already has an adversary. If it doesn't, we must provide one. To accomplish so, add the following nodes:

- **Overview:**

  - IsValid will determine whether or not the Enemy key is set.

  - If it is not set, iterate over all of the presently perceived actors.

  - Cast To BP Muffin will determine whether the actor is a muffin.

  - Whether it's a muffin, see if it's alive.

  - If IsDead returns false, replace the muffin with the new Enemy and exit the loop. '

After clicking Compile, shut AIC Muffin. Play the game, and then generate two muffins, one in front of the other. The muffin at the back will naturally go toward the other muffin.

We will next construct a custom task to cause the muffin to attack.

Developing an Attack Task

Instead of using the behavior tree editor, we may build a task in the Content Browser. Make a new Blueprint Class with the parent BTTask_BlueprintBase.

Open it and name it BTTask_Attack. Incorporate an Event Receive Execute AI node. When the behavior tree performs BTTask_Attack, this node will be executed.

First, we must launch the muffin assault. IsAttacking is a variable in BP Muffin. When the muffin is ready, it will launch an assault. To accomplish so, add the following nodes:

If we continue to utilize the task in its present condition, execution will get stalled. This is because the behavior tree does not know whether or not the job has been completed. Add a Finish Execute to the end of the chain to remedy this.

After that, enable Success. Because we're utilizing a Sequence, nodes following BTTask_Attack will be able to execute.

Our graph should look like this:

- **Overview:**

  - Execute Event Receive when the behavior tree executes BTTask_Attack, AI will be executed.

  - Cast To BP Muffin will check to see if the Controlled Pawn is of the BP_Muffin type.

- If it is, the variable IsAttacking is set.

- Finish Execute notifies the behavior tree that the job has been completed successfully.

- Close BTTask_Attack after clicking Compile.

BTTask_Attack must now be added to the behavior tree. Attack is being added to the Behavior Tree.

- **Launch BT_Muffin:** Then, at the conclusion of the Sequence, add a BTTask_Attack.

- Then, at the conclusion of the Sequence, add a Wait. Set the Wait Time to 2 minutes. This will keep the muffin from attacking all the time.

- Return to the main editor and hit the Play button. As before, spawn two muffins. The muffin will move and rotate toward the direction of the enemy. It will then assault and wait two seconds before attacking again. If it spots another enemy, it will repeat the entire procedure.

The assault and roam subtrees will be combined in the final stage.

Subtree Combination

A Selector composite can be used to merge the subtrees. They, like Sequences, execute from left to right. A Selector, on the other hand, will end when a kid succeeds rather than fails. We may ensure that the behavior tree only runs one subtree by using this behavior.

Open BT_Muffin and add a Selector node after the Root node. After that, link the subtrees as follows:

This configuration will only enable one subtree to execute at a time. Each subtree will function as follows:

- **Attack:** The attack subtree will be run first by the selector. The Sequence will succeed if all tasks are completed successfully. When the Selector detects this, it will cease running. The roam subtree will no longer operate as a result of this.

- **Roam:** The selection will try initially to run the attack subtree. MoveTo will fail if Enemy is not specified. Sequence will also fail as a result of this. Selector will execute its next child, the roam subtree, because the attack subtree failed.

Return to the main editor and hit the Play button. To put it to the test, spawn some muffins.

Why Isn't the Muffin Attacking the Other One Right Away? Every update in a typical behavior tree starts at the root. This implies that it will try the assault subtree with each update, followed by the roam subtree. This implies that if the value of Enemy changes, the behavior tree can quickly change subtrees.

Unreal's behavior trees, on the other hand, do not operate in the same manner. In Unreal, execution continues from the last node that was performed. Because AI Perception does not detect other actors right away, the wander subtree is activated. The behavior tree must now wait for the roam subtree to complete before re-evaluating the attack subtree.

We may remedy this by using the final type of node: decorators.

Developing a Decorator

Decorators, like services, are attached to tasks or composites. Decorators are typically used to perform inspections. The decorator will return true if the result is true and vice versa. We may use this to control whether a decorator's parent can run.

Decorators can also halt the growth of a subtree. This implies that once Enemy is set, we may disable the roam subtree. This allows the muffin to attack an adversary as soon as it detects one.

You may use a Blackboard decorator to use aborts. These merely determine whether or not a blackboard key is set. Right-click on the Sequence of the assault subtree in BT_Muffin. Add DecoratorBlackboard should be selected. The Sequence will now have a Blackboard decorator attached to it.

Then, choose the Blackboard decorator and navigate to the Details section. Change the Blackboard Key to Enemy.

This will check to see if Enemy is enabled. If it is not set, the decorator will fail, resulting in the Sequence failing. This will then enable the roam subtree to function.

We must utilize the Observer Aborts setting to abort the roam subtree.

The Use of Observer Aborts

If the chosen blackboard key changes, observer aborts will abort a subtree. Abortions are classified into two types:

1. **Self:** When Enemy becomes invalid, this parameter allows the attack subtree to abort itself. This can happen if the Enemy dies before the attack subtree is finished.

2. **Lower Priority:** When Enemy is set, this setting will force lower priority trees to terminate. Because the roam subtree comes after the assault, it has a lesser priority.

Change the Observer Aborts setting to Both.

Both sorts of abort will be enabled as a result of this.

If the assault subtree no longer has an enemy, it can instantly move into roaming mode. In addition, when it senses an enemy, the roam subtree can immediately switch into assault mode.

- **Attack Subtree Overview:**

  - If Enemy is set, Selector will execute the attack subtree.

  - If this option is selected, the Pawn will advance and spin toward the enemy.

  - Following that, it will launch an attack.

  - After that, the Pawn will pause for two seconds.

- **Overview of the Roam Subtree:**
  - If the attack subtree fails, Selector will execute the roam subtree. If Enemy is not set, it will fail in this situation.
  - The BTService_SetRandomLocation function will produce a random location.
  - The Pawn will be moved to the randomly created position.
  - It will then wait for five seconds.

Close BT Muffin and then hit the Play button. Make some muffins and get ready for the fiercest battle royale ever.

Behavior Trees

Unreal Engine 4 Behavior Trees assets may be used to generate AI for non-player characters in your projects. While the Behavior Tree component is used to run branches carrying logic, the Behavior Tree relies on another asset called a Blackboard to identify which branches should be performed. A Blackboard acts as the "brain" for a Behavior Tree.

The Blackboard has a number of user-defined Keys that carry information that the Behavior Tree uses to make choices. For example, we might create a Boolean Key named Is Light On that the Behavior Tree may use to determine whether the value has changed. If the value is true, the program may run a branch that leads a roach to escape. If it is false, it may perform a separate branch in which the roach may roam about arbitrarily in the surroundings. Behavior Trees can be as simple as the roach example or as complicated as mimicking another human player in a multiplayer game who seeks cover, fires at other players, and hunts for item pickups.

If we're new to Behavior Trees in UE4, it's a good idea to go through the Behavior Tree Quick Start guide to get an AI character up and running quickly. Suppose we're already familiar with the concept of Behavior Trees from those other applications. In that case, we might want to look through the Essentials section, which includes an outline of how Behavior Trees work in UE4, a User Guide to working with Behavior Trees and Blackboards, and reference pages for the various types of nodes accessible within Behavior Trees.

Creating AI for characters in Unreal Engine 4 may be done in a variety of methods. Blueprint Visual Scripting may be used to command a character to "do something," such as play an animation, move to a particular position, respond when hit by something, and more. When we want AI characters to think for themselves and make their judgments, Behavior Trees can assist.

The Fundamentals of Behavior Trees

Behavior Trees are generated visually, similarly to Blueprint, by adding and linking a sequence of nodes with some functionality to a Behavior Tree Graph. While a Behavior Tree implements logic, a separate asset known as a Blackboard is utilized to hold information (referred to as Blackboard Keys) that the Behavior Tree needs to make educated judgments. A common approach would be to establish a Blackboard, then add some Blackboard Keys before creating a Behavior Tree that uses the Blackboard component.

In UE4, Behavior Trees implement logic from left to right and top to bottom. The numerical sequence of operation is displayed in the upper-right corner of nodes.

Advantages of Behavior Trees

We believe that switching from a finite state machine to a behavior tree has several advantages:

- **Iteration Time:** With a behavior tree, we have modules similar to Lego-blocks, so we can rapidly put together a handful of behaviors and have an AI up and running. Assume you want it to pursue the player. We build a sequence named "Chase Player," rotate it toward the player, set the speed, and lastly instruct it to go, and it will repeat those steps until it is either out of range or meets any other criteria you specify for "Chase Player."

- **Modularity:** As previously stated, we have numerous nodes that serve as the AI's building components. These are the various components that come together to form a functional AI. And the only thing that will restrict what the AI can accomplish is your creativity. And we may set the parameters yourself; for example, in "Chase player," the speed node must be 10, and in "Flee," the speed node must be 20. As we develop individual nodes, everything is isolated from one another, making it adaptable.

- **Structure Like a Tree:** As the name implies, the behavior tree is a tree, which means that each composite node, or root node/sub root node (i.e., Chase player), has branches that have their own nodes, or leaves if we will. That is, each composite node is in charge of its own branches and nodes. This, once again, provides for flexible and decoupled architecture. That is, one composite node may have ten branches for one activity, while another composite node may have two or five. It is entirely up to us to choose how complicated a behavior should be.

CHAPTER 5

Multiplayer Basics

MULTIPLAYER AND NETWORKING

Modern multiplayer experiences necessitate the synchronization of massive volumes of data among a vast number of clients located all over the world. What data you transmit and how you deliver it is critical to creating a compelling experience for consumers since it may significantly impact how your project runs and feels. Replication is the name given to the process of syncing data and procedure calls across clients and servers in Unreal Engine. The Replication system provides a high-level abstraction and low-level customization to make it simpler to cope with the many circumstances that may arise while developing a project for several concurrent users.

OVERVIEW OF NETWORKING

During a multiplayer session, game state information is transmitted between numerous machines over an Internet connection rather than stored alone on a single computer.

DOI: 10.1201/9781003214731-5 **157**

Because transferring information between players is complicated and includes many more stages, multiplayer programming is intrinsically more complex than programming for a single-player game. Unreal Engine consists of a strong networking foundation that runs some of the world's most popular online games, which helps to speed up the process. This article presents an explanation of the principles that drive multiplayer programming, as well as the tools available for constructing network gaming.

Plan Ahead of Time for Multiplayer

If there is a chance that your project may require multiplayer capabilities at some point, you should design all of your gameplay with multiplayer in mind from the outset. If our team regularly follows the different stages for generating multiplayer, the process of producing gameplay will not take much longer than it would for a single-player game. In the long term, our project will be easier to debug and service for the whole team. Meanwhile, any multiplayer gameplay created in Unreal Engine will continue to operate in single-player.

Refactoring an existing codebase without networking, on the other hand, will necessitate combing through the whole project and reprogramming practically every gameplay function. The team members will have to relearn programming best practices that they may have taken for granted up to that time. We will also be unprepared for the technological limitations caused by network speed and stability.

When opposed to preparing for it from the start, introducing networking late in a project is resource-intensive and time-consuming. As a result, unless we are very optimistic that your project will never require multiplayer functionality, we recommend constantly developing it for multiplayer.

Client-Server Architecture

Our game is run locally on a standalone game in a single-player or local multiplayer game. Players link input to a single computer and directly control everything on it. In the game everything, including the Actors, the planet, and each player's user interface (UI), lives on that local system.

Unreal Engine employs a client-server approach in multiplayer network games. One system on the network acts as a servers and conducts a multiplayer gaming session, while the computers of other players act as consumers and connect to the server. The server then distributes game state information to each connected client and allows them to speak with one another.

As the game's host, the server maintains the only genuine, authoritative game state. Next, the server is where the multiplayer game takes place. The clients individually remote-control their Pawns on the server, issuing procedure calls to them to cause them to conduct in-game actions. However, the server does not immediately feed graphics to the clients' displays. Instead, the server duplicates game state information to each client, informing them what Actors should exist, how those Actors should act, and what values certain variables should have. Each client then uses the information to mimic a very near approximation of what is happening on the server.

Example of Client-Server Gameplay

We'll take the example of two players in a multiplayer game to show how this alters gameplay programming approaches. We'll call them Player 1 and Player 2 and walk through the process of having them shoot missiles at each other.

- Player 1 fires a weapon by pressing an input:
  - The Pawn of Player 1 replies by firing its current gun.
  - Any associated sound or visual effects accompany the projectile spawned by Player 1's weapon.

- Player 1 fires a weapon by pressing an input on their local machine:
  - Player 1's local Pawn relays the instruction to fire the gun down to its counterpart Pawn on the server.
  - On the server, Player 1's weapon spawns a projectile.
  - The server instructs each connected client to make a replica of Player 1's projectile.
  - Player 1's weapon instructs each client to perform the sound and visual effects associated with shooting the gun on the server.

- The projectile of Player 1 collides with the Pawn of Player 2:
  - The collision activates a function that destroys Player 1's missile, damages Player 2's Pawn, and plays any associated sound and visual effects.

- In reaction to being harmed, Player 2 performs an onscreen effect.

- On the server, Player 1's projectile advances from the weapon:

  The server instructs each client to mimic the movement of Player 1's shot as it occurs, resulting in their version of Player 1's missile moving as well.

- On the server, Player 1's projectile collides with Player 2's Pawn:

  - The collision activates a code on the server that destroys Player 1's missile.

  - The server instructs each client to delete their copies of Player 1's projectile.

  - The collision activates a function that instructs all clients to play the collision's associated sound and visual effects.

  - The impact of the projectile causes damage to Player 2's Pawn on the server.

  - Player 2's Pawn instructs Player 2's Client to play onscreen effects in reaction to being harmed on the server.

These interactions occur in the same universe on the same computer in the standalone game, making them simple to comprehend and write in literal terms. For example, when you generate an item, you may assume that it will be visible to all players.

These exchanges take occur in multiple separate worlds in the network game: one on the server, one on Player 1's client, one on Player 2's client, and a different world for each other consumer that is participating in the session.

Each planet on each machine duplicates the Pawns, their weapons, and the projectiles they shoot. The server is where the game is being played, but we need to make the clients' worlds appear to have the same activities. To construct a visual representation of the environment on the server, information must be transmitted selectively to each client.

This procedure establishes a distinction between necessary gameplay interactions (collision, movement, and damage), aesthetic effects (visual and audio effects), and private player information (HUD updates). Each of them pertains to a single computer or group of machines in the network. However, copying this information is not automated, and you must define what information gets copied to which computers when you design our games.

The primary issues are deciding what information to duplicate and how to copy it to deliver a consistent experience to all players while simultaneously minimizing the quantity of information replicated to utilize as little network capacity as feasible.

Basic Networking Concepts

The parts that follow go through the ideas that drive network gaming in Unreal Engine. It will provide us with an overview and fast reference to many tools that will assist us in creating our multiplayer games.

Types of Network Modes and Servers

A network mode explains how a computer interacts with a multiplayer network session. A game instance can operate in any of the following network modes:

Network Mode	Description
Standalone	The game is being played as a server, which does not allow connections from distant clients. Any players that take part in the game are all locals. Single-player and local multiplayer games are played in this mode. It will execute both server-side and client-side logic for the local players as needed.
Client	In a multiplayer network session, the game operates as a client linked to a server. There will be no server-side logic.
Listen server	The game is operating in the role of a server, hosting a multiplayer network session. It takes connections from remote users and has local players on the server directly. This mode is frequently employed for both casual cooperative and competitive multiplayer.
Dedicated server	The game is operating in the role of a server, hosting a multiplayer network session. Because it allows connections from remote users but has no local players, it foregoes visuals, sound, input, and other player-oriented features to operate more quickly. This mode is frequently employed in games that need more persistent, secure, or large-scale multiplayer.

Servers are simple for players to set up on their own because any user with a copy of the game may run a listen to a server and play on the same machine. Listen servers are frequently supported by games, which provide an in-game

UI for launching a server or searching for servers to join. However, because the person running a listen server is playing directly on the server, they have the edge over other players who must utilize a network connection to participate, raising questions about fairness and cheating.

They are running as a server, and supporting player-relevant components like graphics and sound adds additional processing overhead. Because of these reasons, listen servers are less appropriate for games in highly competitive settings or games with highly high network loads. Still, they are ideal for recreational cooperative and competitive multiplayer among a small group of players.

Dedicated servers are more expensive and harder to set up, needing a separate computer from each player in a game, complete with its network connection. However, all players who connect to a dedicated server play the game with the same link, ensuring fairness. A dedicated server may process games and networking more effectively since it does not produce visuals or conduct other logic relevant to a local player.

Replicating Actors

The technique of duplicating game state information between various workstations in a network session is known as replication. If replication is configured successfully, the game instances on the separate machines become synchronized. Most Actors do not have replication enabled by default and will conduct all of their functions locally. Set the bReplicates variable in a C++ Actor class or the Replicates setting in an Actor Blueprint to true to allow replication for Actors of a specific class.

The following seem to be the most typical replication characteristics that we will employ to generate networked gameplay:

Replication Feature	Summary
Creation and destruction	When a server generates an authentic version of a replicated Actor, it creates remote proxies for all users connected. The information will subsequently be replicated to those remote proxies. When an authoritative Actor is destroyed, all linked clients' remote proxies are also eliminated.
Movement replication	If an authoritative Actor has Replicate Movement allowed, or bReplicateMovement is set to true in C++, its Location, Rotation, and Velocity will be replicated automatically.
Variable replication	Any variables marked as replicated will be duplicated automatically from the authoritative actor to its remote proxies if their values change.
Component replication	Actor Components replicate as a component of the actor that owns them. Any variables specified as replicated within the component will be duplicated, and any remote procedure calls (RPCs) performed within the component will act consistently with RPCs called in the Actor class.
RPCs	In a network game, RPCs are unique functions that are sent to specified computers. Regardless of the computer on which an RPC is initially invoked, its implementation will only operate on the system for which it was designed. These can be a server (only runs on the server), a Client (only runs on the actor's client), or NetMulticast (runs on every machine connected to the session, including the server).

While famous use cases like creation, destruction, and movement may be handled automatically, all other gameplay aspects cannot be replicated by default, even when enabled replication is enabled. We must specify the variables and functions you wish to reproduce based on the needs of your game.

Several similarities between Actors, Pawns, and Characters do not exist:

- Components of Skeletal Mesh and Static Mesh.

- Materials.

- Blueprints for Animation.

- System of Particles.

- Emitters of Sound.

- Objects of Physics.

Each of these operates independently on each client. However, suppose the variables that control these visual aspects are repeated. In that case, it ensures that all clients have the same information and, as a result, replicates them in roughly the same way.

Role and Authority in the Network

The networking role of an Actor decides which computer controls the actor during a network game. An authoritative Actor is thought to govern that actor's state and will repeat information to other computers in the network multiplayer session. A remote proxy is a small machine's copy of that actor that gets duplicated data from the authoritative actor.

This is recorded via the variables Local Role and Remote Role, which can take the following values:

Network Role	Description
None	The actor does not play a part in a network game and does not replicate.
Authority	The actor is authoritative, and its information is replicated to remote proxies on other machines.
Simulated proxy	The actor is a remote proxy that another machine's authoritative actor controls. Most Actors in a network game, such as pickups, missiles, or interactive objects, will appear on remote clients as Simulated Proxies.
Autonomous proxy	The actor is a remote proxy that can execute some local activities but gets corrections from an authoritative Actor. Autonomous Proxy is often reserved for Actors whom a player, such as Pawns, directly control.

Unreal Engine's default model is server-authoritative, which means that the server always has authority over the game state and consistently replicates information to clients. An Actor on the server should have a Local Role of Authority, and its equivalents on distant clients should have a Local Role of Simulated or Autonomous Proxy.

Ownership by the Client

A PlayerController on a specific client's computer owns pawns in a network game. Any time a Pawn calls a client-only function, it will be directed solely to the machine of the owning player, regardless of which device performs the function. Actors with their Owner variable set to a specific Pawn are associated with that Pawn's owning client and direct client-only functions to their owner's machine. To detect whether or not a Pawn is on its owning client, use the IsLocallyControlled function in C++ or the Is Locally Controlled node in Blueprint.

Priority and Relevance

In a multiplayer game, relevance is used to decide whether or not it is worthwhile to reproduce an Actor. During replication, actors who are no longer regarded as relevant are eliminated. This saves bandwidth, allowing relevant Actors to produce more effectively. If an Actor is not owned by any players and is not physically close to any players, it is deemed irrelevant and does not reproduce. Non-relevant Actors remain on the server and can influence the authoritative game state, but they do not relay information to clients until players are close.

We may manually regulate relevance by modifying the IsNetRelevantFor method, and you can use the NetCullDistanceSquared property to calculate the distance at which an Actor is relevant.

There isn't always enough bandwidth to reproduce all necessary Actors in a single frame of gameplay. As a result, each actor has a Priority value that decides which Actors get to produce first.

Pawns and PlayerControllers have a NetPriority of 3.0 by default, making them the most influential Actors in a game, whereas base Actors have a NetPriority of 1.0. The longer an Actor goes without being successfully reproduced, the higher its priority will get with each succeeding pass until it is copied.

Replication Using Variables

Variables and object references can be replicated using the Replicated or ReplicateUsing specifiers in their UPROPERTY macros in C++ or by marking them as Replicated in the Details Panel in Blueprint. When the value of a replicated variable on an authoritative Actor changes, the information is automatically transferred from the classic actor to the remote proxies linked to the session.

RepNotifies

We may specify a RepNotify function invoked when an Actor successfully receives replicated data for certain variables. RepNotifies only fire when a variable is modified locally, making them a low-cost way to activate gameplay logic in reaction to variable changes on an authoritative Actor. In C++, we may use the ReplicatedUsing specifier in a variable's UPROPERTY macro, or Blueprint, we can change the Replication setting for the variable to utilize a RepNotify.

REMOTE PROCEDURE CALLS

Remote procedure calls (RPCs) are sometimes known as replicated functions. They can be called from any system, but their execution will be directed to a specific machine linked to the network session. RPCs are classified into three types:

RPC Type	Description
Server	This function is only available on the server that is hosting the game.
Client	Only called on the client that owns the actor to whom the function belongs. This logic will not be performed if the actor has no ownership relationship.
NetMulticast	Called on all clients and the server itself that is connected to the server.

Blueprints events and functions can be given the same designations by selecting one of the three kinds accessible in the Replicates selection in the Details Panel.

In C++, we may specify whether a function is an RPC by including the Server, Client, or NetMulticast specifier in its UFUNCTION macro. In their code implementations, they employ the suffix _ implementation.

- **Exampleclass.h**

```
// Server RPC Declaration MyFunction
UFUNCTION(Server, Reliable,
WithValidation)
void MyFunction(int myyInt);
```

- **Exampleclass.cpp**

```
// Server RPC MyFunction
Implementation
void AExampleClass::MyFunction_
Implementation(int myyInt)
{
//Gameplay code
}
```

After identifying a function as an RPC, we may give it gaming logic and call it just like any other function.

Reliability

RPCs must be labeled as dependable or unreliable. By default, functions and events in Blueprint are presumed to be unreliable. We may identify the function as responsible by setting the Reliable option in the Details Panel to true. In C++, the Reliable or Unreliable specifier must be included in every RPC's UFUNCTION macro, along with the function's status as a Server, Client, or NetMulticast function.

RPCs must be labeled as dependable or unreliable. By default, functions and events in Blueprint are presumed to be unreliable. We may identify the function as trustworthy by setting the Reliable option in the Details Panel to true. In C++, the Reliable or Unreliable specifier must be included in every RPC's UFUNCTION macro, along with the function's status as a Server, Client, or NetMulticast function.

Reliable RPCs are assured of reaching their destination and will remain in a queue until successfully received. They are best suited for functions that are vital to gameplay but are not commonly invoked. Collision events, beginning or stopping the fire of a weapon, or spawning Actors are all examples of this.

Validation

The WithValidation specifier specifies that, in addition to an implementation of the function, a function that validates the data of the incoming function call shall be included. This validation function has the same signature as the function for which it is responsible, but it returns a Boolean instead of the original return value. If it returns true, it allows the RPC's Implementation to run, and if it returns false, it prohibits it from running.

- **Exampleclass.cpp**

```
// Server RPC MyFunction Validation
bool AExampleClass::MyFunction_
Validation(int myyInt)
{
    /*
        We don't want MyFunction
Implementation to run if the value of
myInt is negative.
As a result, we return true only if
myyInt is more significant than zero.
    */
    return myyInt >= 0;
}
```

MAKING A MULTIPLAYER GAME IN UNREAL ENGINE

When it comes to developing AAA games, there are few better options than Unreal Engine. This game engine has been incredibly successful in constructing some of the most popular games of the last decade, and with the impending release of a breakthrough version 5, it doesn't appear that this will change anytime soon. With a reputation for excellent visuals and a plethora of speed optimization options, using Unreal Engine development for multiplayer applications is a no-brainer, with a few restrictions.

Is It Challenging to Create a Multiplayer Game on Unreal Engine?

Sure, but not out of reach. The procedure has several intricacies, ranging from establishing fundamental device compatibility to maintaining steady connections and more.

We will only learn about some of them when you come across them in your project, but that won't stop us from attempting to provide us with the remainder of the information we require. We hope it is helpful to your project.

Which Platform Are Ideal for UE4 Multiplayer Development?

With over a dozen systems now supported, cross-platform support is one of UE4's most vital points. However, just because we can write software for a platform doesn't imply it will work for your unique project (e.g., creating a multiplayer shooter in Unreal Engine 4). Let's look at the best solutions for multiplayer projects.

Console/PC

Game consoles and PCs are the best candidates for such projects since they have the highest processing power required to handle UE's high-fidelity graphics and fluid gameplay. You can quickly write software for Windows, Linux, and macOS devices on home PCs. The PlayStation 4/5, Xbox One, Xbox Series X, and Nintendo Switch are the systems on the list. These are the most popular platforms for Unreal Engine FPS multiplayer games.

Mobile

While Unreal may not be the most popular choice for mobile games, it gains traction in large and demanding mobile releases. As of now, the engine supports both iOS and Android development, allowing you to make your product available on billions of devices right now. However, optimizing it and having it function smoothly on less powerful devices is a different story. The essential thing is that whether you use Android or iOS for UE4 mobile multiplayer, you will have all the tools and flexibility you need to succeed.

VR

Unreal has long been a forerunner in virtual reality creation, and its software is compatible with all major VR headsets, including Oculus devices, VIVE, Magic Leap, Valve Index, and PSVR. Choosing the VR multiplayer Unreal Engine standard for your project makes sense because Epic Games has established excellent infrastructure for these devices and because VR headsets are powerful and can fully utilize the heavy and powerful software generated. Aside from that, the program may be used for augmented and mixed reality applications.

Does the Unreal Engine Support Online Multiplayer?

Although HTML5 is one of the platforms supported by UE4, we do not advocate creating a multiplayer game on the web with this software. Unfortunately, Epic Games has not prioritized HTML5 development for its engine, and the present export option is riddled with errors and glitches. It just does not compete with the other web development tools available.

What Game Genres Are Available for Our Unreal Multiplayer Game?

The limitations of UE4 are applied to functionality rather than genre. As a result, we may use the program to develop games of any genre as long as our desired features/logic/mechanics/etc. can be implemented. For example, before creating an Unreal Engine multiplayer racing game suited to this wheel model, we will need to evaluate input compatibility and support.

- Some of the most popular styles in UE4 with samples of each:

  - PUBG.

  - Rocket League.

  - Borderlands 3.

  - Xenon Racing.

Which Is Better for Development: Unreal Engine or Unity Multiplayer?

Unity is UE4's biggest and most famous rival, with a market share of around 45 percent.

Unreal is the winner.

UE4 was designed with multiplayer games in mind, and it has powerful networking technologies that allow us to reach top performance. On the other hand, Unity was designed for smaller tournaments and, in particular, mobile applications. It provides various networking tools (Photon is particularly well-regarded), but its primary solution (UNET) has been abandoned, leaving no fully fledged alternatives. As a result, until Unity provides a new approach, creators will face an additional level of difficulty in configuring networking for AAA products.

What to Expect during the Development Process?

Once we've decided to use UE for your project and have established the tech stack, we'll have to make a slew of decisions that will influence the process. While we can't tell us all there is to know about the MP development process, we can tell you what to expect.

Unreal Engine 4 C++ or Blueprint

When it comes to scripting the game, you have the choice of writing C++ code or using Blueprints (a visual scripting system built into UE4). Most developers choose to utilize C++ as their foundation code and Blueprints for specific portions since it allows them to work faster and flexibly.

Simply mentioned, Blueprints allow you to prototype; construct logic, feedback, and UIs far faster than we could with code.

At the same time, this system is significantly more constrained in what it can accomplish and runs much slower. The more complex the feature, the more difficult it will be to implement in Blueprints. As a result, we may try to discover the optimal combination of the two or stick to C++. We won't be able to construct an online game with Blueprints past the prototype stage.

The Main Difficulties

1. **Artificial Intelligence (AI) design:** Designing a balanced UE4 multiplayer AI for games with non-playable characters or AI opponents might be tough to replace regular competition. On the one hand, we want it to be complicated and clever enough to

challenge players, but not so complex that it overloads their device's processing unit or a server.

2. **Work on core replication:** The synchronization of data across clients and servers is called replication (i.e., the backend communication flow). We'll need to set it up for Actors, Components, and Properties and make the entire system scalable to accommodate variable numbers of concurrent players. This job includes optimizing everything that causes latency, frame rate loss, or packet loss. It's an unavoidable side effect of having matchmaking into multiplayer games in Unreal Engine.

3. **All animations planning:** Many people are unaware of how much the addition of new players influences internal game scenarios and animations. For example, an animation that plays when a player interacts with an object may necessitate the addition of hundreds of other behaviors dependent on criteria such as player proximity, the chronology of who connected with the item first, and how long the thing remains in this new state. In another way, the number of scenarios and animations to plan grows exponentially.

4. **Drawing in a user base:** This is a commercial difficulty rather than a technological one. It requires enormous energy and money to keep MP lobbies running; therefore, a steady supply of players and suitable monetization is necessary to make the project profitable. This entails developing an engaging game with distinct features/plots/mechanics/etc. that players will return to and tell their friends about.

Cost of Unreal Engine Multiplayer

The majority of your expenditures, like with other types of software development projects, will go into paying the wages of developers, designers, quality assurance (QA) engineers, and everyone else engaged with the project. One major issue that will impact the cost is speed how fast the job will be completed. For example, a project created in Blueprints will cost substantially less than a project built in pure C++.

The Unreal Engine multiplayer networking cost will also include maintaining a dedicated server (or numerous servers), licensing software for the models, artwork, and UE4 itself, and investing in hardware on which the game will be tested. AAA titles are not unusual to cost over $1 million only to produce, with hundreds of thousands more merely to maintain and update.

CREATING DEDICATED SERVERS

Unreal Engine's server-client model supports multiplayer network games, with one server functioning as the game's host and players entering the game as clients. The server moderates the actual game state while each player commands their pawns remotely via an independent proxy. The server then duplicates modifications to each connected client, resulting in a very near approximation of the game being played on the server for all participants.

A dedicated server is a server that operates headlessly, as opposed to a listen server, which symbolizes a player running a game on their PC. A headless server does not provide any images, and no one is playing on it locally. This allows a dedicated server to concentrate on gaming logic and to regulate incoming client data, making the most of its resources for hosting a game. Furthermore, this assures a fair playing field for all participants in a multiplayer game. While a listen server is frequently sufficient for casual multiplayer and cooperative play, dedicated servers are suitable for large-scale or competitive games.

This tutorial will walk you through creating and packaging a dedicated server for our multiplayer games.

1. Setup Is Required

To follow the stages in this how-to, your project must meet the following criteria:

- We must be running a source build of Unreal Engine, obtained from Epic Games' GitHub.

  - If our project utilizes an Epic Games Launcher binary build, we must transition it to a GitHub source build.

- A C++ project that supports server-client multiplayer gameplay is required.

  - If we are using a Blueprint project, we must convert it to a C++ project before proceeding.

2. Configuring a Server Build Target

Our project's dedicated servers are a different build target. When we make one, we make a separate executable than when you make the main game. Instead of "TestProjectGame.exe," it would be "TestProjectServer.exe," and opening it would run a dedicated server on our machine.

This section will lead us through adding and building the server build target to our project.

- Open our project's C++ solution. This will be in our project's folder. It's called MyProject.sln in this case.

- Unfold the Source folder in the Solution Explorer and look for the [Project].Target.cs file. This is our project's default build target. An [Project]Editor is also available. The Target.cs file specifies how the Unreal Editor will build for this project. In the same directory, we will construct the server build target.

- In Windows Explorer, navigate to the Source folder. Duplicate [ProjectName]. Target.cs should be renamed [ProjectName]Server. Target.cs. The generated file is named TestProjectServer in our case. Target.cs.

- Return to Visual Studio, then drag *Server.Target. cs from our Explorer window into the Solution Explorer's Source folder.

- Replace the contents of [ProjectName]Server.Target. cs with the following target file instructions:

```
using UnrealBuildTool;
using System.Collections.Generic;


public class TestProjectServerTarget :
TargetRules // Change this line to
reflect the name of our project.
```

```
{
    public TestProjectServerTarget(Tar
getInfo Target) : base(Target) //
Change this line to match the name of
our project
    {
        Type = TargetType.Server;
        DefaultBuildSettings =
BuildSettingsVersion.V2;
        ExtraModuleNames.
Add("TestProject"); // Change this
line to reflect our project's name.
    }
}
```

- Locate our project's .uproject file in its root directory, then right-click it and choose to Generate Visual Studio Project Files. This will rebuild our game's Visual Studio solution and locate our *Server.Target. cs file.

- Select the Development Editor to build configuration from the drop-down menu.

- Build our solution by going to the toolbar and selecting Build > Build Solution. We may also accomplish this via the Solution Explorer window's context menu.

- Build the solution again using the Development Server build setup.

- Locate the Binaries/Win64 folder in our project. Inside this folder, we should see Server files, including [ProjectName]Server.exe.

3. Configuring Entry and Default Maps

To test our dedicated server, we must configure our project's default maps so that the server can run a playable game and people may connect to it. There are several approaches to achieve, but the most straightforward is incorporating the connection flow right into the user's entry map when they launch the program.

- Launch Unreal Editor and open your project. Make sure to move all Level files to a Content/Maps folder within the Content Browser. This may be accomplished by copying the ThirdPersonCPP Maps folder into the main Content folder.

- Make a new level called [ProjectName]Entry, where [ProjectName] is the name of our project. It will be named TestProjectEntry in this case. We can start with a blank map as our starting point.

- Open the Entry map first, followed by the Level Blueprint script. Add an Open Level node to the BeginPlay node and set its value to 127.0.0.1. This is our local IP address, which means we're instructing the game to connect to a server on our computer. If we replace this value with a legitimate IP address, we will connect to a server at that address.

- Open the ThirdPersonExampleMap and remove the default third-person character from the level. Instead, ensure that the group has two PlayerStarts. This will guarantee that gamers have a consistent launch experience when they connect.

- Open our Project Settings, go to project > Maps and Modes, and expand the Default Maps. Replace them with the following:

Parameter	Value
Editor startup map	[Project-Name]Entry
Game default map	[Project-Name]Entry
Transition map	None
Server default map	ThirdPersonExample-Map

This ensures that the server navigates immediately to ThirdPersonExampleMap, while users guide to the Entry map and connect to the server.

4. Our Project's Packaging

- To access our packaging options, go to file > Packaging > Packaging Settings.

- By pressing the rectangle button with an arrow at the bottom of the Packaging section, we may access the advanced options.

- Locate the Maps List to Include in a Packaged Build and include our Entry map and ThirdPersonExampleMap.

- Choose a directory to package our project by going to file > Package Project > Windows (64-bit). Our output folder is TestProject/Packaged in this case.

- Select file > Package Project > Build Target from the menu. Along with the standard build target, we should see [ProjectName] Server. Choose this option.

- Package the project once more, using the same output folder as previously. Along with WindowsNoEditor, there should now be a folder named WindowsServer.

5. Launching and Testing Our Dedicated Server

Finally, it's time to put our dedicated server to the test.

- Locate [ProjectName]Server.exe in the WindowsServer folder we created in the previous section. It's named TestProjectServer.exe in this case.

- Make a shortcut to Server.exe, change the name, and append "- ThirdPersonExampleMap" to the end. We've renamed it TestProjextServer.exe - ThirdPersonExampleMap in this case.

- Open the server shortcut's properties by right-click-ing it. Add "-log" to the end of the Target field and press Apply. This will cause the dedicated server to display a log-in command prompt when we exe-cute it. Because we configured the server to open to ThirdPersonExampleMap in the previous sections, there is no need to provide map parameters to this shortcut.

- To start our dedicated server, double-click the short-cut. A command prompt window with an output log will appear. If the server is successfully launched, we will see output at the bottom indicating how long it took to bring up the level.

- Double-click TestProject.exe in the WindowsNoEditor folder. It will open the game in a new window and appear to take you straight to ThirdPersonExampleMap.

- To exit the game window, press ALT+Tab, then run TestProject.exe to start a new game instance. If it is successful, the player will appear in the window we started. We may also look at the server log to determine if both players connected to the server.

BLUEPRINTS MULTIPLAYER

Unreal Engine 4 comes with many multiplayer capabilities out of the box, and it's simple to create a basic Blueprint game that runs over a network. It's simple to get right in and start playing multiplayer. The built-in networking functionality in the Character class and its CharacterMovementComponent, which the Third Person template project utilizes, is responsible for most of the logic required to do essential multiplayer work.

Examining the Gameplay Framework

To add multiplayer functionality to your game, we must first grasp the functions of the engine's primary gameplay classes and how they interact with one another—especially in a multiplayer context:

- PlayerController.

- GameInstance.

- GameState.

- PlayerState.

- Pawn.

- GameMode.

More information may be found in the Gameplay Framework documentation; however, keep the following principles in mind while building our game for multiplayer:

- The GameInstance exists throughout the life of the engine's session, which means it is generated when the engine starts up and is not deleted or replaced until the engine terminates. On the server and each client, a distinct GameInstance exists, and these instances do not communicate with one another. So the GameInstance exists outside of the game session, and it is the only game structure that persists across level loads. It is an excellent place to store persistent data, including lifetime player statistics (e.g., the total amount of games won), account information (e.g., locked/unlocked status of unique items), or even a list of maps to rotate through in a competitive game like Unreal Tournament.

- The GameMode object resides solely on the server. It usually holds game-related information that clients do not need to know explicitly. For instance, if a game includes unique rules such as "rocket launchers only," the clients may not need to see this rule. Still, when randomly generating weapons throughout the map, the server must learn to choose only from the "rocket launcher" category.

- Because the GameState resides both on the server and on the clients, the server may utilize replicated variables on the GameState to keep all clients up to current on game data. GameState replication is excellent for information relevant to all players and viewers but is not connected with anyone unique. A baseball game, for example, may use GameState to reproduce each team's score and the current inning.

- Each client has one PlayerController for each player on that system. These are mirrored between the server and the linked client but not between other clients, therefore the server has PlayerControllers for all players while local clients only have PlayerControllers for their local players. PlayerControllers live as long as the client is connected and is associated with Pawns, but they are not killed and respawned as frequently as Pawns are. They are well-suited to exchanging information between clients and servers without repeating that information to other clients, including the server instructing the client to ping its minimap in reaction to a game event detected only by that player.

- Every player who is engaged to the game, on the server and on the consumers, will have a PlayerState. This class can be used for duplicated attributes relevant to all clients, not just the owner client, such as an individual player's current score in a free-for-all game. They, such as the PlayerController, are linked to specific Pawns and are not destroyed and respawned when the Pawn is.

- Pawns (including Characters) will exist on the server and all clients, and they can consist of duplicated variables and events. It depends on the scenario whether we utilize the PlayerController, the PlayerState, or the Pawn for a given variable or event, but keep in mind that the PlayerController and PlayerState will continue as long as the current player stays linked to the game. The game does not load a new level, whereas a Pawn may not. For instance, if a Pawn dies during gaming, it is usually destroyed and replaced by a new Pawn; however, the PlayerController and PlayerState remain connected with the new Pawn once it has finished spawning. The Pawn's health would thus be saved on the Pawn itself, as it is unique to the Pawn's instance and should be reset when the Pawn is replaced with a new one.

Replicating Actors

Actor replication is at the heart of UE4's networking technology. When an actor's "Replicates" flag is set to true, it will be synced from the server to clients connected to that server. It's critical to realize that actors are only replicated from the server to the clients; actors cannot be duplicated from the client to the server. Clients must, of course, be able to communicate data to the server, which they do through replicated "Run on server" events.

Authority

One of the connected players is regarded to have control over every actor in the globe. The server has control over all actors on the server, including any duplicated players. Consequently, when the Has Authority function is called on a client and a cloned actor is used as the target, it throws an error. The Switch Has Authority convenience macro may also quickly branch for different server and client behavior in replicated actors.

Variables

A Replication drop-down in the details panel of variables on our actors allows us to choose how and whether our variables are duplicated.

Option	Description
None	This is the default setting for new variables, and it signifies that the value will not be communicated to clients over the network.
Replicated	This variable will be sent to clients when the server duplicates this actor. The receiving client's variable value will immediately change so that the next time it is accessed, and it will reflect the value on the server. Of course, while playing over a real-world network, the updates will be delayed by a time factor determined by the network's latency. Remember that replicated variables may only flow one way: from the server to the client! See the "Events" section for information on sending data from a client to the server.
RepNotify	The variable will be reproduced in the same way as in the Replicated option, but an OnRep <variable name> function will be added to our Blueprint. When the value of this variable changes, the engine will automatically run this function on both the client and the server. We are allowed to implement this function in whatever way we see fit, as our game needs.

Spawning and Elimination

When a replicated actor is generated on the server, clients are notified, and they will likewise spawn a copy of that actor. However, because replication does not go from client to server in general, if a replicated actor is generated on a client, that actor will only live on the client that spawned it. The server or any other client will not copy the actor. The spawning client, on the other hand, will have power over the actor. This is still beneficial for aesthetic actors who have no impact on gameplay. Still, for actors that do affect gameplay and should be copied, it's preferable to ensure they are generated on the server.

When destroying duplicated actors, the scenario is similar: if the server removes one, all clients will delete their corresponding copies. Clients are free to eliminate actors over whom they have power, i.e., actors they created themselves because they are not copied to other players and affect them. The request is rejected if a client attempts to destroy an actor over whom they do not have permission. The crucial idea here is the same as when creating actors: if you need to kill a duplicated actor, do it on the server.

Replicating an Event

Blueprints allow us to perform events across clients and servers in addition to duplicating actors and their variables.

Ownership

When working on multiplayer, especially with duplicated events, it's critical to identify whose connection is deemed to be the owner of a specific actor or component. For our purposes, keep in mind that "Run on server" events may only be triggered by actors (or their components) owned by the client. Typically, this implies that you can only send "Run on server" events from the actors listed below or from a component of one of them:

- The PlayerController of the client.

- A Pawn owned by the client's PlayerController.

- The PlayerState of the client.

Similarly, if a server sends "Run on owning client" events, such events should be triggered on one of these actors as well. Otherwise, the server will have no idea which client to deliver the event to, and it will only run on the server.

Events

We may choose how if at all, our custom events are reproduced in the details panel.

Option	Description
Not replicated	This is the default, and it indicates that this event will not be replicated. If invoked on a client, it will only execute on that client; it will only run on the server if invoked on a server.
Multicast	When a multicast event is triggered on the server, it is duplicated to all connected clients, regardless of which connection owns the target object. If a client begins a multicast event, it will be considered if it was not duplicated, and it will only be executed on the client who started it.
Run-on server	If we call this event from the server, it will only run on the server. If it is invoked from a client with a target owned by the client, it is replicated and executed on the server. Clients provide data to the server primarily through "Run on Server" events.
Run-on owning client	If this event is called from the server, it will be executed on the client that owns the target actor. Because the server can hold actors, an "Occur on Owning Client" event may run on the server despite its name. When a client invokes an event, it is regarded as if it isn't duplicated, and it only runs on the client who summoned it.

The tables below show how the various replication mechanisms impact an event's execution, depending on how it is initiated.

Because generic actor replication is supposed to be server-to-client only, sending a replicated event from the client to the server is the only way to transfer client information. It is also essential to understand that multicast events may only be transmitted from the server. Because of Unreal's client-server approach, a client is only linked to the server and not to any other clients. As a result, a client cannot deliver a multicast event directly to the other clients and must instead connect with the server.

We may, however, mimic this functionality by using two replicated events: one Run on server event and one Multicast event. If desired, the Run on server event implementation can validate before calling the multicast event. The multicast event implementation would carry out the logic that wants to run for all connected players.

Considerations for Join-in-Progress

When utilizing replicated events to transmit game state changes, consider how they interact with a game that allows join-in-progress. When a new player enters a game already in progress, any repeated events that occurred before the join are not executed for the new player. The message is that synchronizing essential gameplay data via replicated variables is ideal if we want our game to operate correctly with join-in-progress.

A typical pattern is that a client does some action in the world, tells the server about the action through a "Run on server" event. The server modifies certain replicated variables based on the activity in the implementation of that event. The result of the action is then visible to other clients who did not conduct the movement through the replicated variables. Furthermore, any clients that join in progress after the action has been completed will see the right state of the world since they obtain the server's most recent value of the replicated variables. If the server had just sent an event, the join-in-progress players would have been unaware of the activity.

Reliability

We can select whether a repeated event is Reliable or Unreliable.

Reliable events are assured to arrive at their destination (provided the ownership requirements outlined above are fulfilled), but they require additional bandwidth and, perhaps, delay to do so. Avoid delivering reliable events too often, such as every tick, because the engine's internal buffer of dedicated events may overflow, causing the related player to be disconnected.

Unreliable events do precisely what their name implies: they may not reach their destination, for example, if there is packet loss on the network or if the engine thinks there is much higher-priority traffic it has to transmit. As a result, faulty events consume less bandwidth than reliable events and may be called more frequently.

MAKING USE OF STEAM SOCKETS

Steam Sockets is a networking plugin that uses the new Steam network protocol layer, which is supported by Unreal Engine as of Steamworks SDK version 1.46.

This plugin, as compared to the earlier SteamNetworking protocol, delivers enhanced security and dependability by utilizing Steam's communication network, with built-in distributed denial-of-service (DDoS) protection, end-to-end encryption, and NAT traversal. Steam Sockets also calculates ping for listening to servers, which matching systems can utilize to match users to servers with better performance. This is a significant advance over SteamNetworking, which could not calculate ping until users had already connected to a server.

Turning on the Steam Sockets Plugin

The following actions may be taken to enable Steam Sockets for Windows, Mac, and Linux-based builds:

- In Unreal Editor, open your project and go to Edit > Plugins.

- Click the Networking plugins group under Built-in Plugins in the Plugins Menu.

- Locate and enable the Steam Sockets plugin. For the modifications, you must restart Unreal Editor.

Using Steam Sockets Functions

Config options for activating and removing large-scale functionality can be used to configure Steam Sockets.

OnlineSubsystemSteam.bUseSteamNetworking determines whether or not the SteamSockets SocketSubsystem is the default subsystem. By default, the value is true. Most projects will not require this parameter to be changed, and it is primarily provided as a backward-compatibility option for developers moving from the prior SteamNetworking protocol.

When utilizing a dedicated server, OnlineSubsystem-Steam.bAllowP2PPacketRelay determines whether or not packets should tunnel over the Steam communication network. By default, this value is true. When this option is turned off, dedicated servers reveal their connection addresses directly, allowing for customized implementation. When this option is selected, dedicated servers operate via Steam's relay network, protecting them from DDoS assaults and improving security. Regardless of this option, peer-to-peer (P2P) listen servers always use Steam's communication network.

GRAPH OF REPLICATION

The Replication Graph Plugin is a network replication mechanism for multiplayer games intended to scale effectively with high numbers of players and replicated Actors. For example, Epic's Fortnite Battle Royale begins each game with 100 connected players and around 50,000 cloned Actors. The conventional network replication technique, which requires each duplicated actor to decide whether or not to deliver an update to each connected client, performs poorly in such instances and would choke the server's CPU.

Solutions such as separating Actors into staggered groups or updating less regularly may alleviate the problem, but they may also worsen the client experience by reducing update frequency. The Replication Graph removes the need for Actors to examine each connected client separately, resolving the CPU performance issue without compromising the client experience.

Structure

The Replication Graph is made up of Replication Graph Nodes, which are in charge of constructing lists of Actors to replicate to each client on demand. Data may be saved across several frames and transferred between client connections since this system is made from permanent objects rather than function calls executed by the replicated Actors themselves. Because of this unlimited, shared data, the Replication Graph system can reduce its time to generate replication lists for each client.

Replication Graph Nodes (abbreviated "nodes") perform the actual job of determining which Actors may require updates, grouping them, storing precomputed lists to deliver to clients, and so on. Their ultimate goal is to give "replication lists" of Actors on demand to each client connection as rapidly as feasible so that the server uses as few CPU cycles per actor per client as possible.

Each node can perform a distinct function, and developers are invited to create new nodes for their games as needed. Nodes can be game-agnostic or use game-specific information. Placing Actors in particular nodes based on their function in your game allows you to have more control over how and when they reproduce. Building additional nodes and utilizing the Replication Graph to allocate Actors to the best nodes possible based on how they behave in your game will result in the most significant reductions in server CPU time spent on network replication list preparation.

Activating the System

In one of two approaches, you may set up our project to utilize a custom Replication Driver (the parent class of Replication Graph):

- In the "DefaultEngine.ini" file, provide a Replication Driver class.

- Binding a function to the default Replication Driver's creation Delegate that returns an instance of your Replication Driver class.

Configuration Files (.ini)

Open the "DefaultEngine.ini" file for your project to specify the Engine's default Replication Driver. Find (or create) the [/Script/OnlineSubsystemUtils.IpNetDriver] section and set (or create) the "ReplicationDriverClassName" element to the name of the Replication Driver (or Replication Graph) class you want to use. This should essentially look like this, with "ProjectName" replaced with the name of our actual project and "ClassName" replaced with the name of our custom class:

```
[/Script/OnlineSubsystemUtils.IpNetDriver]
ReplicationDriverClassName="/Script/
Project_Name.Class_Name"
```

In Code Binding

Binding to a Delegate allows us to generate the proper Replication Driver for the current game mode or map in code if our project has many game modes or maps with dramatically varying networking needs. To utilize this approach, attach a function named CreateReplication-DriverDelegate to the UReplicationDriver function. Our bound function must return a valid instance of our chosen Replication Driver class, as demonstrated by the following lambda function:

```
UReplicationDriver::CreateReplicationDriver
Delegate().BindLambda([](UNetDriver*
ForNetDriver, const FURL& URL, UWorld*
World) -> UReplicationDriver*
{
return NewObject<UMyReplicationDriverClass
>(GetTransientPackage());
});
```

High-Level Illustration

For a game with a large number of connected clients and an even more significant number of synchronized Actors, a Replication Graph that distributes Actors to various nodes based on type and state can save a considerable amount of CPU time. This enables the creation of games that would be impossible to create using typical replication approaches. To handle its massive amount of replicated Actors and connected clients, a game of this magnitude may construct a Replication Graph and Replication Graph Nodes with the following features:

- **Divide Actors into groups depending on location:** For games in the battle royale, MOBA, or MMORPG genres, the world can be split into grid spaces, or specified rooms or zones for dungeon crawlers or corridor-style first- or third-person shooters, or any manner that matches our game's play areas. Adding Actors to each grid cell or room from which the actor might be seen or heard would allow the node to supply the client with the endless Actor list for whatever grid cell or room the client's camera is in, resulting in a faster client update.

- **Identify "dormant" Actors and keep a separate list of them:** While certain Actors, such as those portraying players or AI-controlled characters, are likely to require regular updates, many Actors may be pre-placed in the level and will not move or change state unless a player interacts with them. Without sending a network update, these Actors may go for an extended period (perhaps the whole game session).

  For example, in Fortnite Battle Royale, people and missiles are intended to update until they are eliminated from the game continually. On the other hand, a tree is supposed to sit inactive for an extended period, requiring no updates from any client. When the tree is harmed, each client who can see it must be kept up to date. Finally, after the tree is destroyed, every client that receives the update detailing the tree's demise is no longer required to receive additional information about the tree.

- **If our game's characters can pick up and carry items, make sure to update those goods with their carriers:** When a player pulls out a thing or weapon and carries it about, or wears a piece of clothing or armor, but the actor representing the item (assuming it is a distinct Actor and not just a Component) to a specific category that only changes when the owning player updates, and never otherwise.

- **Create a list of exceptional Actors well-known to all clients:** Special Actors that are always network-relevant to every player and may be placed in a single node that records these Actors, keeping them out of other lists where they can use CPU cycles doing a needless calculation.

- **Make a list of exceptional Actors who are always (or seldom) relevant to specific clients:** Individual individuals or teams of players might each have their always-relevant list node. This is especially important for ensuring that a player's teammates are constantly up to date or that opponents "exposed" via a unique in-game detection power remain visible to the person who disclosed them. If the "reveal" period expires, these Actors can be re-added to their default nodes.

Make the most excellent use of your server's CPU time by creating a Replication Graph that intelligently distributes Actors to different nodes depending on the actor's role inside the game. The ultimate result is consistent server performance for games that would otherwise be unplayable on current hardware. The Replication Graph Plugin comes with several Replication Graph Node classes used in large-scale online games. Developers are also invited to create unique node classes depending on their understanding of the inner workings of their particular game.

TRAVELING IN MULTIPLAYER MODE

- Travel can be seamless or non-seamless:

  There are two types of travel in UE4: seamless and non-seamless. The primary distinction is that seamless travel is a non-blocking operation, whereas non-seamless travel is blocking.

  When a client makes a non-seamless journey, the client will disconnect from the server and reconnect to the same server, with the updated map loaded.

  When feasible, it is suggested that UE4 multiplayer games employ seamless travel. It will often result in a more pleasant experience and prevent any problems that may arise throughout the reconnecting procedure.

- A non-seamless journey must take place in three ways:

  - When the map is loaded for the first time.

  - When connecting to a server as a client for the first time.

  - When we wish to quit a multiplayer game and begin a new one.

Three primary functions motivate people to travel: APlayerController::ClientTravel, UWorld::ServerTravel, and UEngine::Browse When deciding which one to use, they might be a little perplexing, but here are some tips that should help:

- **UEngine::Browse**

  - When loading a new map, it's similar to a hard reset.

  - This will always result in a non-seamless journey.

  - As a result, the server will disconnect existing clients before proceeding to the target map.

  - Clients will be removed from the current server.

  - The map must be local because dedicated servers cannot connect to other servers (cannot be URL).

- **UWorld::ServerTravel**

  - Only for the server.

  - The server will be moved to a new world/level.

  - All linked clients will do the same.

  - This is how multiplayer games go from map to map, and the server is responsible for calling this function.

  - For each client player who is connected, the server will call APlayerController::ClientTravel.

- **APlayerController::ClientTravel**

  - When invoked from a client, it will connect to a new server.

  - When called from a server, it instructs the specific client to travel to the new map (but stay connected to the current server).

Allowing for Uninterrupted Travel

To allow smooth travel, you must first create a transition map. The UGameMapsSettings::TransitionMap field is used to configure this. This variable is empty by default, and if your game leaves it blank, an open map will be constructed for the transition map.

The transition map exists because there must always be a world loaded (which contains the map), and we can't release the old map before loading the new one. Because maps may be pretty huge, having both the old and new maps in memory simultaneously would be a horrible idea, which is where the transition map comes in.

So we may now move from the current map to the transition map and from there to the final map. Because the transition map is so tiny, it adds little extra overhead while overlapping the current and last maps.

After we've created the transition map, we'll need to set AGameModeBase::

UseSeamlessTravel to true, and seamless travel should function from there.

Effortless Travel Flow

When conducting seamless travel, the following is the usual flow:

- Mark the performers who will make it to the transition level.

- Make our way to the transition level.

- Mark the actors who will make it to the final level.

- Make our way to the last level.

Performance and Bandwidth Suggestions

It might take a long to replicate actors. The engine does its best to be as efficient as possible, but you can do a few things to help.

When gathering actors for replication, the server will consider relevance, update frequency, dormancy, and so on. We can change any of these tests to improve performance. When considering how to make this procedure as efficient as feasible, prioritize as follows:

- Setting replication to false (AActor::SetReplicates(false)).

  - When an actor isn't replicating, they aren't on the list in the first place; therefore, this is the most significant win; actors who don't need to reproduce are labeled as such.

- Reduce the NetUpdateFrequency value.

  - The fewer often an actor updates, the shorter the time it takes to update. It's ideal for keeping this figure as low as feasible. This value reflects the number of times per second that this actor will replicate to clients.

- NetClientTicksPerSecond.

- Dormancy.

- Relevancy.

If a property isn't essential, don't mark it to duplicate. When feasible, attempt to extract state from existing duplicated characteristics.

Make use of the quantization capability that is currently available. FVector NetQuantize, for example. These will considerably minimize the size required to duplicate this state to clients, and if utilized correctly, should result in no visible artefacts.

Because "FName"s are not often compressed, when using them as arguments to RPCs, take in mind that they will generally send the string each call. This can represent a significant amount of overhead.

Appraisal

Unreal Engine 4.27 is a comprehensive set of development tools for game development, architectural and automotive visualization, linear film and television content generation, broadcasting and live event production, training and simulation, and other real-time applications.

Unreal Engine 4 is a set of game production tools that can create everything from 2D mobile games to AAA console blockbusters. It powers games like ARK: Survival Evolved, Tekken 7, and Kingdom Hearts.

For novices, developing with Unreal Engine 4 is relatively straightforward. We can construct complete games with the Blueprints Visual Scripting system without writing a single line of code. We can rapidly get a prototype up and running by combining it with an easy-to-use interface.

The Unreal Engine End User License Agreement for Creators is a legal agreement that we agree to when joining the Unreal Engine via one of two typical methods. It controls our usage of the Unreal Engine and specifies your rights and responsibilities while creating projects with the engine. This license is completely free and royalty-free;

DOI: 10.1201/9781003214731-6

we may use it to build internal or free projects and linear content or custom projects for customers but not to publish off-the-shelf services.

We may launch projects on Windows PC, PlayStation 5, PlayStation 4, Xbox Series X, Xbox One, Nintendo Switch, Google Stadia, macOS, iOS, Android, AR, VR, Linux, SteamOS, and HTML5. The Unreal Editor is available for Windows, macOS, and Linux.

Registered developers for their particular platform may access PlayStation 5, PlayStation 4, Xbox Series X, Xbox One, Nintendo Switch, and Google Stadia console tools and code at no additional cost.

Is the Unreal 4 Engine Open Source?

Unreal Engine is free for everyone, and all future releases will be free as well.

We may use the engine for everything from game creation to education, architecture, visualization, and VR, cinema, and animation. We pay a 5% royalty on gross income after the first $3,000 per product each quarter when we ship a game or application. It's a straightforward agreement in which we prosper only if we succeed.

This is the whole technological stack that Epic used while developing our games. It ranges from small projects to high-end blockbusters, supports all major platforms, and contains the C++ source code. Our objective is to provide us with everything we need to do anything while remaining in control of our schedule and destiny. Whatever we need to construct and deploy our game can be found in UE4, sourced from the Marketplace, or built from scratch and then shared with others.

What Is the Purpose of Unreal Engine?

The firm said that Epic Games' Unreal Engine 4, the most recent version of its gaming engine, is now entirely free for anybody to use.

Epic first released Unreal Engine 4 in March 2014 for "early adopters" on a subscription basis, costing $19 per month plus a 5% royalty charge on sales. Previous generations of the Unreal Engine were aimed at huge development teams producing high-budget games, with the technology requiring expensive license costs. Epic stated at the time that it wished to make Unreal Engine 4 available to a broader audience.

The free software includes the complete C++ source code for Unreal Engine 4, and it has Windows PC, Mac OS X, Android, iOS, virtual reality (Oculus Rift and Gear VR), Linux, SteamOS, and HTML5. Registered PlayStation 4 and Xbox One developers can also use those devices.

Benefits of Unreal Engine

- Unreal Engine is capable of handling a wide range of projects.

- Unreal Engine is particularly good at shooters.

- Epic gives us access to the source code.

- Unreal Engine is available for free.

- Unreal Engine enables rapid development and iteration.

- Blueprint simplifies Unreal Engine for non-technical personnel.

- The Unreal Engine is excellent for large-scale games.

- The Unreal Engine lowers the barrier to cross-platform development.

- Unreal Engine has a comprehensive toolset as well as a powerful editor.

- Unreal Engine facilitates recruiting.

- Unreal Engine has excellent official and community support.

- The Marketplace in Unreal Engine is well-stocked.

- Because of its performance tracking, Unreal Engine is ideal for VR.

Its documentation is a little hazy, and it does not have as large a community as Unity. Some scary interfaces, not to mention the fact that the coding language is C++.

It provides a gaming engine that is a powerhouse, pushing visuals to the utmost level while being efficient. Unreal is jam-packed with features and capabilities, and once mastered, there will be no limit to achieving your idea.

With Epic's recent attempts to make Unreal more accessible with the introduction of Blueprints (visual coding system), ongoing work to enhance documentation, instructional content, and a significant emphasis on community building, Unreal is a good choice for any game developer.

- **Unreal graphics:** Equivalent effects CAN be obtained with both engines. On the other hand, Unreal is jam-packed with tools and presets that work straight out of the box and can be readily modified.

- **You name it:** volumetric lighting, post-production, lens flares, and so on. Everything is there, ready to use, and looks lovely from the time we put it in.

When compared to Unity, the lighting in Unreal appears to be considerably more realistic and fluid. When we bake the lighting in "Production Quality," it looks fantastic, with very few, if any, graphical flaws or weird artifacts.

Shadows have a beautiful falloff and a finished appearance. All of this while requiring substantially fewer draw calls than Unity, resulting in significantly improved speed.

It also has a fantastic material editor, allowing one to build and change materials using the node graph effortlessly. It operates like those of other 3D software such as Maya or 3DS MAX. This allows us to adapt and iterate based on live input within Unreal quickly.

Post-processing is entirely integrated and ready to use, providing a wide range of options for grading, lens flares, volumetric effects, etc.

The technology is identical to that used in the film, giving it a seamless cinematographic impression.

We may also add trigger volumes across the globe so that when a player enters that volume, the colors change. For example, to a more chilly blue, allowing you to change the tone for different locations on your map, and so on.

Jobs with the Unreal Engine

- Software Tester
- Epic Games
- Unreal Engine Developer

- Physics Programmer
- Gameplay Programmer
- Game Tester
- Software Engineer
- Unreal Engine Generalist

Unreal Future is a great place to start if we want to work with interactive 3D.

There has never been a better or more exciting time to be a maker. Jobs are changing, and new occupations are developing in every area as a result of technological advances.

One of the inventions poised to revolutionize the world we live in is real-time technology. Dynamic 3D powers the games we play, the films we enjoy, and the virtual worlds we live. The technologies that power Fortnite also assist architects in seeing buildings before they are created and doctors in simulating a challenging surgery before touching a patient.

In the future, interactive 3D will enhance our ability to develop, invent, and communicate. It has the potential to change whole sectors and perhaps our economies.

Learning Unreal Engine and interactive 3D abilities puts you at the cutting edge of technological innovation and artistry, preparing us for the fascinating careers of the future. Unreal Futures is a major learning series in which beginners may study hands-on from leading business veterans and build a project in Unreal Engine.

We've teamed with specialists from industry leaders to provide a once-in-a-lifetime opportunity to learn from the best. This series introduces students to the interactive 3D business, illustrates how Unreal Engine works, and delivers an engaging experience that mimics an exciting real-world project.

Is Unreal Suitable for Beginners?

For novices, developing with Unreal Engine 4 is relatively straightforward. We can construct complete games with the Blueprints Visual Scripting system without writing a single line of code. We can rapidly get a prototype up and running by combining it with an easy-to-use interface.

Is It Worthwhile to Study Unreal Engine 4?

Working for gaming companies means you won't be asked if we know Unreal or any other engine. Understanding how to deal with engines is easy compared to knowing how to create anything and do it in any engine you're given. However, it is unquestionably worthwhile to learn.

Index

Printed in the United States
by Baker & Taylor Publisher Services

Printed in the United States
by Baker & Taylor Publisher Services